Heaven, Hell and Paradise Lost

Heaven, Hell

and *Paradise Lost*

ED SIMON

PUBLISHING

New York, NY

Ig Publishing
Box 2547
New York, NY 10163
www.igpub.com

ISBN: 978-1-63246-152-0

PRINTED IN THE UNITED STATES OF AMERICA

FIRST EDITION | FIRST PRINTING

To
Anne, Mary, and Deborah

Book I—Sin

Of Mans First Disobedience, and the Fruit
Of that Forbidden Tree, whose mortal taste
Brought Death into the World, and all our woe.

—*Paradise Lost*, Book I

I want to do right, but not right now.

—Gillian Welch,
"Look at Miss Ohio"

After aimlessly walking about Bloomsbury on an intermittently rainy afternoon, I unsuccessfully decided to search for the grave of John Milton while nursing a wicked hangover, or as is probably more likely, while still being drunk from the previous evening. Only my second week in London, I was supported with a modest graduate stipend for my research at the British Library, mornings spent at that modernist building with the red-brick facade not far from the Victorian ostentation of King's Cross Station, requesting four- and five-hundred year old books brought to me by pleasant librarians at concerningly efficient speed. Obscure books such as the Puritan-minded Anglican divine William Crashaw's *A Sermon preached before the right honorable the Lord Lawarre, Lord Govoernour and Captaine Genrall of Virginea . . . Feb. 21, 1609* and the Scottish New World speculator William Alexander's epic poem, "Doomes-day." Every evening, however, since I'd arrived from Philadelphia, I'd started at the pubs while the sun was still out, because what else could be expected with the unnervingly late northern dusk? Pint after pint of real ale at the Queen's Head not far from the library; drams of Jameson's at The Boot; Guinness at Miller's across from the train station and, when feeling homesick and slightly patriotic, Sam Adams at the Old Red Lion Theatre Pub. As A. E. Housman wrote in that most English of poetic cycles, 1896's *A Shropshire Lad*, "malt does more than Milton can / To justify God's ways to man."

Ostensibly here to transcribe sixteenth and seventeenth-century books that endowed geographical discoveries with apocalyptic significance, the majority of my nights were either spent at the theater or getting horrendously shit-faced, blackout drunk. If I knew what pub my nights started at, I rarely remembered where they ended, though by the good graces of Something I was always able to stumble back mostly safely into the University of London dorm which I rented for an amazingly cheap price. That summer, London suffered through an uncharacteristic heat wave, and the thin-blooded British hadn't outfitted any of the dorms with air-conditioning, while all the windows were suicide-proof, making respite impossible and requiring several cold showers a day just to regulate body temperature. On top of that, my room looked directly into Joseph Grimaldi Park, named after the nineteenth-century master of pantomime who is entombed there. Hot, sweaty, drunk, and watched over by the spirit of a dead clown—July, 2013. Not that

London made me drink—I drank when I was back in Bethlehem, Pennsylvania, where I was getting my PhD, and I drank when I was in Pittsburgh where I was from. I drank in New York and I drank in Philly, I drank in Dublin and I drank in DC, I drank wherever I happened to be. I drank, because I'm an alcoholic, and it's what I do—what I did. And, even with several years of hard-fought sobriety (which has immeasurably improved my life), I can still say with a dark measure of pride that when it came to drinking, *I was damn good at it.*

That summer I'd also been accepted at a conference on the sexy topic of seventeenth-century hymn translation, and the spectacularly wealthy jewelry magnate who funded my fellowship out of a sense of nostalgic largesse for his undergraduate institution nestled in the hills of the Poconos was happy to pay the registration fee so that I could talk about the *Massachusetts Bay Psalter* in the cloistered, stone medieval halls of Queen Mary's University near the Carthusian priory built in 1371 atop a mass burial ground of bubonic plague victims from a generation before. This being my first international conference, and suffering from that affliction of impostor syndrome that in honesty deserves to strike any scholar worth their muster, I was already a bit tender when my talk didn't go well. The argument of my presentation, as best as I can recall it, was that the *Massachusetts Bay Psalter* was interesting. Not the best or most important or most scintillating of claims, for sure, and yet for some reason the conference organizers had accepted it. Then the Q&A—*Was I aware of the reception history of Sternhold and Hopkins as regards psalm translation in colonial New England?* I was not aware of the reception history of Sternhold and Hopkins as regards psalm translation in colonial New England. *How could you make a claim of influence in prosody between Sidney's renditions and those in Massachusetts without more evidence?* I don't know how I could make that claim of influence in prosody between Sidney's renditions and those in Massachusetts without more evidence.

I'm a graduate of an inner-city public high school, and I can recognize when I'm being made fun of; I know when the mood switches from rigor to rancor. The men—it was largely men (and large men) who were uniformly white—came from programs at Oxford and Cambridge, Edinburgh and St. Andrews, while they'd misspelled my university as it appeared on my name tag. Sanctimonious malignancy often marks scholars at their most pernicious, where solemn mockery only understood by seven people on earth obscures any of those higher values we ostensibly mouth platitudes about. Rather than truth, or even better curiosity, what the Golden Children actually valorize is pure and raw competition. Poor, nasty, brutish, but never short and certainly not solitary. Dejected and suffering from a low blood-alcohol level, I wandered throughout Islington, trying to trick myself into thinking that the presentation hadn't gone badly while pounding Carlings and Carlsbergs, when I ran into another conference-goer, an Oxbridge British grad student also in his late twenties, and also a Miltonist.

I can't remember his name, or even what he looked like, though when I envision that night I see somebody out of a nineties Brit Pop band, an insufferably posh toff with longish straight dirt brown hair and a corduroy jacket. After discussing his research with a celebrated professor whose work I had to read while studying for my doctoral comprehensive examination, I asked him about my talk. The posh toff laid into me, how bad it was, how terrible American standards must be. I recall that he ended his monologue with a snaggletoothed smirk. So blasé he had been, so cavalier the whole display had been, that I was shocked that he didn't even think twice about such bluntness. It was cruelty for itself, mocking just to mock. He didn't care—that's what had been insulting. I excused myself to the bathroom, at the top of a rickety, chipped wooden set of steps centuries old, the linoleum inside a grimy chess board of white and black, the sink stained with yellow detritus. I splashed water on my face several times, and as I've repeated this story as a joke so many times it has begun to take on the appearance of a truth, I now remember that when I looked back up at the mirror my reflection was already there, facing forward, smiling, and letting me know—giving me permission—for what I thought I needed to do. Having walked up that narrow staircase shakily I now descended in confidence, inviting the posh toff out for another drink, the first of his many stupid decisions.

At the Earl of Essex and the Compton Arms, the Lexington and the Lord Clyde, we drank liquor with liquor chasers, at the House of Hammerton and the Draper's Arms, the Old Queen's Head and the Martyr of Sutphen, we had beer after beer, ale after ale. The whole time he continued to talk about his research, the ways he was revolutionizing Milton studies, the difference between Americans thinking that they could understand immaculately British verse and the English for whom it was their birthright. He made a bit out of my last name, though by this point my paranoia may have been outstripping my observational clarity. He began to slur about how terrible American beer was, how Yanks thought that they could drink but were always so sloppy. By the time we were at Martyr of Sutphen, behind its freshly painted red door and those wooden framed windows with thickly spackled black trim, a few sad spider plants in flowerpots underneath the bubbled opaque glass that made darkness visible, I convinced him to have a final drink with me before last call. Shifting uncomfortably on the high bar stools at a little back table underneath a black-and-white picture of some ancient Arsenal team and a faux-gilded framed painting of a stocky bulldog, the posh toff admitted that he was worried about how his adviser's affections had shifted to more promising, younger colleagues; how he had stalled not only in his research but more worryingly in his writing; how so much was dependent on his giving a good talk the following morning, a schedule which I had assiduously memorized.

I nodded with understanding, shook my head with empathy, furrowed my brow with what looked like real feeling. With some sheepish embarrassment, he admitted that he didn't know London all that well—this city that I'd first visited fifteen years before—in a nation that I once lived in—and since he felt unsteady on his feet, would I help him back to his lodging? Gathering the posh toff up from his underarm, we made our way out of the Martyr of Sutphen into London's neon gray haze as I guided this young scholar back toward the hostel that he'd checked into after arriving at King's Cross a few days before. Somewhere in Angel, I even held the posh toff steady while he vomited in a puddly alleyway. Finally, bringing him back to the front door of the slightly disreputable hostel, and barely conscious or aware of how he'd even gotten there, he suddenly seemed to realize with some horror that his presentation was only eight hours into the future. "Good luck," I whispered, and when he looked up and finally saw the blinkered hate in my eyes, I swear on everything that is unholy that he totally understood what I'd consciously done to him that night, as I turned around and with straight precision made a perfect walk back home.

The subject of all great literature is either about redemption or its loss. Soteriology—that is the branch of theology that concerns itself with salvation—is the only worthy topic of prose, poetry, or drama. Whether you take any of that God stuff literally or not is irrelevant to this discussion. Noble, heroic, and good people corrupted or degenerated; sinful and wicked men made whole—either/or—those are the narratives which should concern any genuine art, because the turmoil within an individual mind, the canker and possible curing of the soul, is the only drama commensurate with the broken, flawed, limited, damning, painful, horrible, and beautiful experience of being trapped in a human body and a human life. Nathaniel Hawthorne's *The Scarlet Letter,* Leo Tolstoy's *Anna Karenina,* Charles Dickens's *Great Expectations;* Milan Kundera's *The Unbearable Lightness of Being,* Ian McKewan's *Atonement,* and William Faulkner's *Absalom, Absalom!* Dickens's bildungsroman may be heavy on plot (and words), the orphan Pip gifted treasure by a mysterious stranger, the iciness of beautiful Estella and the cruelty of mad Miss Havisham in her moldering mansion and her rotting wedding dress, but fundamentally the book is about salvation. Faulkner's novel details the legacies of Southern ambivalence about history, Quentin Compson in his Cambridge dorm haunted by the Civil War and obsessed with miscegenation, yet fundamentally it's about sin. What differentiates soteriological literature—which is to say great literature—from mere story is that the former takes seriously the question of whether an individual life's decisions can be justified, and that's the only ethical question worth our consideration. Not to treat these questions didactically, but to explore ambivalence and ambiguity in the cursedness of life, to understand morality as an issue of what it means to be alive. Anything less and a story is mere video game. We are infinitely complex, unknown even to ourselves, and soteriological literature reflects that. As Marilynne Robinson writes in the hauntingly beautiful *Gilead*, every "single one of us is a little civilization built on the ruins of any number of preceding civilizations."

Few poets ever quite ascended to the fullest encapsulation of this theme like Milton in his 1667 epic *Paradise Lost*, ostensibly an account of Satan's fall during the War of the Rebel Angels, his invasion of the Garden of Eden, and his tempting of Eve and Adam with fruit from the Tree of Knowledge of Good and Evil. What it's really about is the disease of the soul, humanity's strange and awful predicament of being a poetic ape strung between heaven and hell on this debased earth. *Paradise Lost* takes as its subject what the great Church Father St. Augustine described in his fourth-century *Confessions*, writing that he "loved to excuse my soul . . . it was my impiety that I had divided me against myself. That sin then was all the more incurable because I did not deem myself a sinner." A distinctly premodern view, the idea of being a "sinner." Indiscretion and transgression can be reduced by sociology and psychology, perhaps even further by biology and chemistry, regulated with drugs and therapy. When Augustine's "original sin" is discussed today, it's often as some archaic, prudish, reactionary neuroticism; most people assume that it only has something to do with sex. What Augustine says is rather all the more profound—that there is something deeply wrong with us. Not an optimistic evaluation, yet as the apologist G. K. Chesterton astutely noted in *Orthodoxy*, original sin "is the only part of Christian theology which can really be proved." Jesus Christ is the second coequal, coeternal, consubstantial divine person of the Holy Trinity, hypostatically unified in the incarnation and suffering death for the world's redemption. *The hell is that?* You're naturally wicked. *Seems about right.* Why did I do what I did to the posh toff? *Because I could.*

"Any moderately perceptive and reasonably honest observer of humanity has to acknowledge that we are remarkably prone to doing bad things—and, more disturbingly, things we *acknowledge* to be wrong," writes Alan Jacobs in *Original Sin: A Cultural History*, and though the essayist's Reformed Protestant beliefs are distant from my own, I can't help but agree on this particular topic. "Of man's first disobedience," Milton writes in his epic's first words, describing his subject in a single audacious sentence that erupts with that glottal Big Bang of a proposition sounding as if the first syllable ever spoken, and that then unspools in byzantine grammar and labyrinthine syntax across sixteen enjambed lines, with fifteen commas, twelve dependent clauses, a colon and semicolon, all before culminating in the declaration that he shall pursue "Things unattempted yet in

Prose or Rhime." Joe Moshenska argues in *Making Darkness Light* that the opening of *Paradise Lost* has a "conspicuous strangeness," marked by "long and highly complicated sentence structures ... running the sense of the words across several lines, ... stretching of the norms of English grammar to its limits," arguing that Milton's goal is that this "vast and complicated poem refuses to be experienced as a whole." If Milton has engendered a constant criticism it's that despite his ability to turn a phrase, *Paradise Lost* is not an easy read. That's the point, for Milton's poem isn't interpreted, it interprets you. Taking as his subject "man's disobedience," his chewy verse is deliberately difficult because no other subject is as complicated as humanity's willing evil. Theodicy, the branch of theology that concerns itself with why evil things happen to good people, which reached its greatest expression in the biblical book of Job, is the only other subject of which worthy moral literature can be written. *Paradise Lost*'s central topic is just as disquieting—why do average, normal, typical men and women choose to do evil? Why are all of us, at some point or another, drawn to hurting ourselves, to hurting other people?

This is Milton's major preoccupation, but *Paradise Lost* is neither prescriptive nor didactic, for as in with all great moral literature, including the Bible, the epic is not some self-help guide. The poet's intention is to hold within his mind's focus the disunion and disorder that marks humanity. Disunion, disorder, disquiet, disruption—that is all which wickedness really is. Milton had a certain yet intangible understanding that our world is irrevocably fucked; the comprehension that our own propensity to such chaos, whether we call it original sin as Augustine did or like Sigmund Freud we call it Thanatos, means that in an intrinsic way we're deeply fucked as well. No person is so saintly that they never yell at telemarketers, never flip the bird to people who cut them off in traffic, never reply to an idiotic social media post with bile and invective. "These are the most truistic of truisms," writes Jacobs, "and I can't imagine that anyone would deny them, but they raise questions, do they not? . . . Where does this wrongdoing come from?" Few have ever argued that the world itself is perfect; that's the Panglossian dictum of advocates for the status quo; maybe slightly more have claimed that there is a perfectibility to humanity, but normally those who hold to such a faith ascribe it to themselves, and they're the ones most at risk. Answering Jacob's question, or Milton's, or Augustine's, or the apostle Paul's, normally finds recourse in Genesis, wherein the traditional interpretation has original sin being imparted unto humanity after the first couple disobeyed God's commands concerning that forbidden fruit and were subsequently expelled from Eden. Augustine's doctrine bares similarity to others' observations about creation's fallenness—Jewish kabbalists such as the sixteenth-century Sephardic poet and rabbi Isaac Lauria understand our universe as being born out of a divine fracturing, while the Vedic traditions of Hinduism and

Buddhism see corruption in the poisonous illusions of maya. We can't, and shouldn't, reduce complex and singular religious beliefs across millennia and continents into original sin; nirvana isn't heaven, the Qur'an isn't the Bible, and a rabbi isn't a priest, but it's not inconsequential that most major traditions acknowledge that humans can't help but do bad things.

For all of the cinematic drama of *Paradise Lost* (incidentally the only canonical work that has never been adapted for film), including the war in heaven, the expulsion of that fallen horde into the sulfury depths of Hell and the demons' subsequent construction of their terrible and awesome parliament Pandemonium, and the revelation of cosmic secrets from the celestial and magnificent archangel Raphael, it can be easy to overlook that the poem's denouement is somebody eating an apple. To chew is to fall, to masticate is to perish. From that apple (though Genesis isn't specific) came sin. Read as a "Just So" story, it's foolish. But on a level beyond even the mere allegorical, the significance of this transgression is inescapable. To the "Why?" of this issue, Milton added his own innovation that expanded on Genesis, a type of biblical fan fiction. In Book II of *Paradise Lost*, as Lucifer travels through the undifferentiated Chaos which separates Hell from earth, he encounters a fish-scaled female monstrosity, an ever mercurial being who shifts in and out of different shapes, a "Goddess arm'd / Out of they head I sprung ... All th' host of

Heav'n back they recoild afraid / At first, and call'd me *Sin.*" From conjugal incest, Satan and his daughter Sin produced a new progeny who would be known as *Death,* with Lucifer unable to remember any of these twisted events that made such demons possible. An evocation of Hera's birth from Zeus's brow, Milton not only impugns the classical pagan tradition by associating the Olympian gods with Christian demons, but he effectively marries Athens with Jerusalem, Greece with Judea, the Hellenic with the Hebrew, crafting a syncretic mythopoeic system that addresses the grotesquerie of sin, the way such malignancy can erupt from our minds.

Did Milton think that this is what really happened? Almost certainly not, but regarding Genesis, it's the wrong question. Modern atheists and Christian fundamentalists are united in how they read the Bible, with the latter simply believing it and the former not. Epistemologically and hermeneutically (I promise not to speak too much like that), where the first word refers to the study of how we know things and the second to how we interpret them, Milton was neither concerned with if such things "actually" happened nor did he think that these narratives should be read "literally." Neither *Paradise Lost* nor the Bible describe the world as it actually exists, but rather they describe the soul as it experiences that world. Their language is poetic, not scientific. "And when the woman saw that the tree was good for food, and that it was pleasant to the eyes, and a tree to be desired to make one wise, she took of the fruit thereof, and did eat, and gave also unto her husband with her; and he did eat," reads Genesis 3:6. Did such a thing actually happen somewhere along the banks of the Euphrates and Tigris, was it that fatal choice that's the reason why your boss chews you out, why your friends gossip about you behind your back, why I am incapable of drinking like a normal person? Of course not. Nothing about this story is factual, and yet it's true. Mere facts and profound truths are two entirely different things. Interestingly enough it was the actual filching of fruit that at least inspired the doctrine of original sin, but in the form of pears rather than apples. Augustine describes his Carthaginian youth, when he and some friends in that dusty Roman frontier town of Hippo stole some pears from a neighbor's tree and then threw them to the pigs, writing that he had "no motive for my wickedness except wickedness itself. It was foul, and I loved it. I loved the self-destruction, I loved my fall." That's why your boss chews you out, why your friends gossip about you, why I can't drink. Because Augustine's "act had no point— that it was inexplicable and gratuitous—was precisely the point," writes Stephen Greenblatt in *The Rise and Fall of Adam and Eve*. Greenblatt observes that "What seemed like nothing turned out to be everything."

Paradise Lost's is both anatomy and taxonomy of wickedness and wrongdoing, written not in the idiom of logic but through the vocabulary of mythopoesis. If almost every religious tradition understands disharmony as our tribulation, than Christianity's singular theological contribution was to focus that universal observation into a singular intensity. "I was seeking not to gain anything . . . but shame for its own sake," as Augustine wrote. When *Confessions* was penned, it was far from a given that anything like belief in original sin would become *de riqueur* for Christians. Augustine was writing in response to a theologian in Briton named Pelagius, who believed that salvation was merited entirely through moral works alone. Sometimes misunderstood as the gentler position, Pelagius's theology allowed for absolutely no slip-ups of any kind, so that his was an exhausting belief whereby the vast majority of humans would condemn themselves to Hell for chewing out employees, gossiping, and drinking to excess. Ironically, Augustine's doctrine is surprisingly more humane, an embrace of the understanding that we're all fallible, imperfect, and frequently wrong. The claim that humanity is depraved, and that faith, works, grace, or some combination of these is necessary in the struggle against perdition, is Christianity's most enduring influence, for other faiths believe that gods are capable of incarnating as men, other religions hold that redemptive sacrifice is required, and every other sect has some variation on the sublimely stated platitudes of the gospels. *But original sin is original.* By the time that Milton was writing *Paradise Lost,* Western Christianity was embroiled in intense debates about sin— what's the degree of human agency in being able to choose or not choose evil actions? Do we have the free will in our salvation? Or are redemption and damnation predestined by God?

Because the Latin-speaking Augustine was never particularly venerated among the Greek-speaking Orthodox, the arguments concerning original sin were a preoccupation primarily in Western Europe, first among Catholics and then Protestants. Historian Diarmaid MacCulloch jokes in *All Things Made New: The Reformation and Its Legacy* that the "sixteenth-century Reformation was a battle in the mind of fourth-century Augustine." The Reformation warred over any number of theological questions—free will and faith, works and worship, episcopacy and the Eucharist—but sin and the will were arguably the most personal of these. Martin Luther's second article in the *Augsburg Confession* reiterates that "all men are full of evil lust and inclination from their mothers' wombs and are unable by nature to have true fear of God and true faith in God," though as with the Roman Catholic Church baptism can wash the stains of original sin away. Austere John Calvin repeated this sentiment in his 1536 *Institutes of the Christian Religion*, concluding that original sin "seems to be a hereditary depravity and corruption of our nature, diffused into all parts of the soul, which first makes us liable to God's wrath," concurring with the most radical implications of Augustine's thinking that had been rejected by the Catholic Church at the Council of Orange a millennium earlier in 529. Calvin maintained that nothing we do merits salvation, that only God's freely given grace distributed among a limited number of undeserving people assures that Heaven isn't completely empty. "Total depravity," the rather punkish sounding designation for the first of the five principles which defines Calvinism (the others are "unconditional election," "limited atonement," "irresistible grace," and "perseverance of the saints," all memorized with the handy mnemonic of "TULIP") holds that every one of us is in bondage to sin, slave to our own basest desires and only capable of holding it together with the assistance of God. Early modern disputations about soteriology are sometimes simplistically reduced to being disagreements among free will believing Catholics and predestination adhering Protestants, but lines between denominations could be ambiguous. French Catholic Jansenists for example, from which the poetic mathematician Blaise Pascal derived many of his beliefs, adhered to an understanding of predestination and sin every bit as stern as Calvin's, while the followers of the Dutch Protestant Jacob Arminius (known as "Armininians") allowed for a degree of human agency. Such baroque debates were more than just scholarly disagreement in an era of violent religious war, but in the midst of this was Milton, who despite his stated purpose remains ambiguous in terms of his own position.

"O goodness infinite, goodness immense!" enthuses Adam in the final book of *Paradise Lost,* "That all this good of evil shall produce,/And evil turn to good; more wonderful/Than that which by creation first brought forth / Light out of darkness!" When the reader finishes, they discover that in a crucial way the first man, and perhaps Milton, thinks that the fall and the expulsion from Eden was actually *good*. Milton believed that humanity is forever tarred by the actions of the first couple, and that sin is a metaphysical darkening of our souls, an inclination toward pride, gluttony, lust, avarice, envy, sloth, and anger. Far from simply being an issue of rule-following, "Law can discover sin, but not remove it," as he writes. Which is precisely why Milton thinks that the fall was good, because it necessitated the incarnation of Christ, an abundantly greater good than just two people living in perfection in the garden for an eternity. This heterodox doctrine known as "felix culpa," or "fortunate fall," allows for both an awareness of humanity's debasement, but that then allows for a type of new freedom— now capable of not just choosing bad, but also choosing the good, for they are finally differentiated with the knowledge imparted from that tree. The measure of the blessed can only be taken with the particulars of the damned. As Augustine wrote in *Enchiridion,* "For God judged it better to bring good out of evil than not to permit any evil to exist."

There is much that I'm ashamed of, a seeming universe of it, yet I've always been grateful to be an alcoholic. In recovery the rock bottom is our felix culpa, the portal through which the active addict loses the illusions which so often confuse falling for flying. When it comes to all of the creeds of Christianity, of the Athanasian and Nicene, and the brutal debates which marked Milton's era between Catholics and Protestants, Arminians and Calvinists, I'm at best ambivalent—but I certainly believe in original sin. Malt taught me that more than Milton did. Inheritor of a secular, liberal worldview that serves me well in the majority of circumstances, I nonetheless couldn't yoke rationality to alcohol in any way that improved my life. All of those rules you invent—I'll drink two drinks quickly, and then only one an hour after that; only beer, no liquor; you can only drink at home; a glass of water for every drink you have. Every single one of those rules broken, sometimes on the first try. "We admitted we were powerless over alcohol—that our lives had become unmanageable," reads the first step of twelve—just like the number of books in *Paradise Lost*—from the immaculate, polyphonic, multivocal, hard-boiled epic of original sin compiled by Bill W. in 1939 and officially titled *Alcoholics Anonymous* but everywhere known simply as the "Big Book." In prose more reminiscent of Mickey Spillane than Milton, the Big Book presents dozens of stories of women and men—rich and poor, Black and white, religious and agnostic—who suffered from a compulsion, a madness that made them do the same thing over and over again, then their fall, and eventual redemption. That powerlessness is as acute an experience of original sin as I've ever experienced, the knowledge that once I get that one drink I can't stop till I've had all of them. No logic can really make me stop, even though I can't assure my own safety, even though I would wake up on sidewalks or in the hospital, and always with the gaping black abyss of that which I simply called "The Fear." And yet I'm grateful for all of it—that which reminds me I'm fallen, I'm a human.

Wandering through London—mouth dry, head pounding, hands shaky—past pubs that I might have drank in, cobble-stoned alleyways that I could have walked down, lurid red royal mailboxes that I possibly pissed on. There was no real goal to my perambulations, buffeted about like the souls of the lustful in Dante's *The Divine Comedy*. If my time that summer was divided between the library, the theater, and getting shit-faced, then my final activity was the slightly fussy hobby of visiting famous writers' graves. So far, I'd seen the common hovel at St. Nicholas in Deptford far south of the Thames where Christopher Marlowe was buried in 1593 after he was stabbed through the eye over an argument involving a tavern bill, the environs of the churchyard dark and melancholic. A little after that, I'd explored the crypts underneath the magnificent domed St. Paul's Cathedral, examining the modest plaque affixed near where Sidney was entombed after felled by a bullet at the battle of Zutphen, the zealous Protestant coming to the Dutch's aid in their war against the Spanish. And I found the statue of John Donne in repose, a marble depiction of the great poet in his funeral shroud as he imagined he would appear on Judgment Day, "When my grave is broken up again." Discovered in a pile of rubble after the original cathedral burnt during that hideous conflagration of 1666 when the capital was reduced to ash, the feet of Donne's marble are charred with exhaust, appearing as if the poet had been dangled over inferno for just a bit. Milton would finish *Paradise Lost* the year after.

Now, with hair-of-the-dog in my future, I decided to visit Milton's grave at St. Giles-without-Cripplegate, the unfortunate name of his parish church derived from the Medieval entrance to the city that the lame were required to use. The church was now in the midst of the brutalist Barbican Center, a bestial behemoth built upon the neighborhood destroyed by the Luftwaffe. A handsome if modest gray-stoned structure, St. Giles was framed by these dystopian environs, an ancient Roman wall visible a few hundred yards beyond, the original foundations of Londinum uncovered not by archaeologists but by German incendiary. Approaching the church—sweaty, tired, and confused—and the doors were locked. Searching for Milton, and I couldn't find him. Stumbling again, and a few blocks away I arrived at Bunhill Fields, where nonconformists and dissenters were buried, a solemn green space of tightly packed gravestones, the final resting place of Daniel Defoe and John Bunyan. And there, perpendicular to the mass of the head stones, was the modest grave of Milton's greatest reader, the prophetic visionary and mystical Romantic poet William Blake. "The road of excess leads to the palace of wisdom," Blake wrote in his 1793 *The Marriage of Heaven and Hell*, in large part about Milton's antinomian energies, about the fortunate fall that takes us through perdition before we can get to paradise. I sat on a bench next to Blake's grave for about the space of a half an hour, before I went off to find an eye opener. I drank for two more years after that. It couldn't be helped for a while. I'd missed the posh toff's presentation, still passed out on the floor of my dorm, with no clue if it went well or not. These days, I hope that he did all right. Mostly.

Book II—Life

One fatal tree there stands, of Knowledge called,
Forbidden them to taste. Knowledge forbidden?
Suspicious, reasonless. Why should their Lord
Envy them that? Can it be a sin to know?

—*Paradise Lost,* Book IV

He had read much and knew what books could
teach; but he had mingled little in the world, and
was deficient in the knowledge which experience
must confer.

—Dr. Johnson, *Lives of the Poets*

Bulldozers razed the building where I first read *Paradise Lost*. McIlvaine Hall was demolished some three years after I had been a student in the survey course required of all English majors, in which I chose not to pay attention to discussions about *Beowulf* and Geoffrey Chaucer's *The Canterbury Tales*, but rather to absentmindedly flip the bible paper of *The Norton Anthology of English Literature* and thus to surreptitiously learn of Satan's travails through Chaos, Raphael's revelation of cosmic secrets, and the first couples' exile from Eden. My C+ in British Literature was abundantly and unreservedly earned. McIlvaine had been constructed in 1897, a red-brick shell encasing a dark wood interior with a green-domed clock tower added several decades later, a theater unused for years the inert heart of the building, with bits of water-damaged spackle collecting in damp white crumbles and pipes freezing over in winter. Once a biology laboratory, several of the classrooms had the fading lettering of "Botany" and

"Zoology" still visible on the heavy dark-stained wooden doors, everything converted into English classrooms a generation before. A faintly Lovecraftian aura, the ghosts of experiments past that seemed to linger in rooms where we read Shakespeare and Austen but where once cephalopods had been dissected. So threadbare did the building seem by the time I attended—nostalgia aside, most of us understood why it was torn down—that it felt like McIlvaine creaked beneath you, that it was an organic being, and the respiration which you sensed was its death rattle. That at night the staircase and the floorboards, the doors and their jambs, shifted about uncontrollably; that in violation of physics the interior of the building was larger than the exterior. This was where I first read of Milton's Hell.

Nestled in the Alleghenies where steel gave way to coal and the mill towns filled with Catholic immigrants transformed into mining towns populated by Presbyterians, Little Washington (as it was called by locals) was only a click above the Mason-Dixon Line, but just barely. McIlvaine was on the campus's eastern edge, the back of it's white-washed trim looking out over the aluminum and wood-paneled homes of the working class neighborhood which abutted the train tracks, it's yellow-faced clock chiming over the pristine quadrangle that had at its center a memorial to the students who'd died in the Civil War, the cenotaph commemorating about two-thirds Union deaths and the remainder Confederates who'd attended this college only a few miles from the Pennsylvania border with what had then been Virginia. Of those three conflicts—the English Civil War, the American Revolution, and the Civil War—the same perennial themes were engaged: royalists against republicans, liberty against obedience. And in each circumstance, the correct side won, though not without cost and not without revanchism, as Milton understood. Technically the eleventh oldest college in the United States, and thus frustratingly absent from the *U.S. News and World Report* listings that commemorated the most venerable institutions of American higher education, Washington & Jefferson had been founded by Princeton Theological Seminary students John McMillan, Joseph Smith, and Thaddeus Dodd in 1787 as a Presbyterian school for the Indians, the school's official mythologizing detailing how the men set out from New Jersey across the Appalachians, with the first founder's pewter mush spoon exhibited in a library display case. Older than both the Constitution and the French Revolution, founded just a bit more than a century after Milton was entombed at St. Giles, hauntings were thick among these Gothic environs. My professor described McIlvaine in a post uploaded to the college website as a place "creaking around bits of discarded, dark years."

That archaism extended, in the best of ways, to curriculum. Not that the school was particularly traditional—it wasn't. And not that in our English classes we didn't talk about Michel Foucault and Paul Lacan—we did. Yet in an institution that had missed the "Theory Wars" which marked the humanities in the 1980s and 90s, the largest disciplinary debates weren't between old-fashioned formalists and post-structuralists, but between those who focused on British literature versus those who specialized in American. Out-of-time, really (in all senses of that word). "English rose rapidly at the end of the nineteenth century and in the first decades of the twentieth," explains Robert Scholes in *The Rise and Fall of the English: Reconstructing English as a Discipline.* "Its decline began after mid-century and now threatens to accelerate." As an undergraduate, I had no awareness of this unfortunate fall; that would take years of adjuncting as a poorly paid contingent faculty member. English was still king, and Milton was very much on the docket. Something slightly fussy and old-fashioned about it all, which was to the benefit those who graduated having read *Paradise Lost.* Furthermore, since so much of where you first encounter literature affects your relationship to that work, these archaic environs founded by those Presbyterian ministers (a denomination that Milton had some political allegiance toward, for a bit) freezing on the Allegheny plateau as they headed toward the direction of the Ohio territory assisted me in identifying *Paradise Lost* as not just an epic, but a tragedy and a romance, a utopian meditation and a horror story, a fever dream and an intoxicant.

What I mean by this, is that while sitting in an

uncomfortable seat, hearing the clank of the radiator during those low winter sun afternoons of a Pennsylvania February, squibs of light radiating over the frosted grounds, made for an appropriate atmosphere to take Milton on his own terms— ancient and prophetic, complicated and befuddling, strange and beautiful. Turning the tissue paper of the Norton, my back aching years earlier than it should as my spine contorted into the splintery wooden chair that looked more like a Shaker antiquary than modern classroom furniture, I could examine pictures of Milton included within. The portrait made of him when he was a student, twenty-one years old in 1629 and a pale, effeminate young man with long brown locks who either affectionately or with some tongue-clucking was known as the "Lady of Cambridge." The William Faithorne engraving of 1670, a middle-aged Milton rendered in stark black-and-white chiaroscuro, now wrinkled and with exhausted eyes that have witnessed Revolution, Interregnum, and Restoration, appearing every bit the Puritan of our imagination in austere black cloak, but still with the beautiful hair. The life-size bronze sculpture that marks Milton's place of final repose, and beneath it the corpse itself, exhumed by grave desecrators from St. Giles who wished to verify that it was the poet within, confirming his identity because clinging to his bony pate were still those wisps of gorgeous hair, then taking the opportunity to pry lose a shin bone or a jaw that latter appeared for sale at markets throughout London, the

Protestant polemicist converted into something akin to a Catholic saint, as now he was the secular equivalent of "rags, then relics, beads ... The sport of winds."

The course was taught by a requisitely tweedy professor with a limitless ability to quote from memory, whether *Sir Gawain and the Green Knight* or *The Tempest,* and whatever disservices I committed as a student were more than compensated with what was the beginning of this odd relationship with *Paradise Lost.* I hadn't arrived at Washington & Jefferson with any aspirations to be a nascent Miltonist, though with a much-thumbed but rarely used black Moleskin and a pair of Chuck Taylors that I'd used a purple pen to link the opening lines of Allen Ginsburg's "Howl" around the rim of white rubber where the sole hits the black canvas, I did harbor pretensions to being a writer. Stolid liberal arts school that W&J is, English majors were surprisingly common. Our course catalogue listed at least three single-author classes, respectively dedicated to Chaucer, Shakespeare, and Milton, with the second course sometimes divided between the playwright's comedies, histories, and tragedies. Anecdotally, my impression is that the Milton course was the least popular, offered at strange times in the summer session or early in the morning. Chaucer had connotations of mead-swilling pilgrims in mottled pants and jester hats weaving their way to Canterbury, bawdy stories about cunnilingus and tavern wenches; Shakespeare was, remains, and forever shall be Shakespeare, but Milton? In many peoples' estimation you'd do as well to read something by the guy on the Quaker Oats box. In a discipline long and correctly criticized for its perseveration on words by old, dead, white guys, Milton was proverbially the oldest, deadest, and whitest of guys. Even Dr. Johnson in his estimable *Lives of the Poets* would write in 1779 that *Paradise Lost* was a book which a "reader admires and lays down, and forgets to take up again."

Milton has had a complicated place in the cannon precisely because he's not that much fun. *The Canterbury Tales* and Shakespeare's folio are undeniably such, they still read as fresh, and as a playwright the latter naturally lends himself to film adaptation. Though both Chaucer and Shakespeare—and everybody else in the British canon from Jane Austen to Charles Dickens, Lord Byron to Charlotte Bronte—was deeply enmeshed in the rituals of the church, the language of scripture, and the insights of theology, Milton naturally seems more Christian than all of them (for good reason). Chaucer and Shakespeare lived in an overwhelmingly religious culture, where to even countenance agnosticism or atheism was an intellectual impossibility, but since they didn't perseverate on theological questions they seem more secular, so that ironically Milton, the latest of the three, feels as if he's the earliest. A bit of a paradox, for in many ways Milton is neither archaic nor modern, ancient or contemporary, but rather of the gloaming period, a creature of both the past and the future who composed a massive epic in a language of his own invention that gestures toward political, religious, and cultural issues that are shockingly current. Nigel Smith argues in his provocatively titled study *Is Milton Better than Shakespeare?* that "there are certain ways in which Milton is more salient and important . . . because he is a poet who places liberty at the center of his vision." Encountering Milton among the Alleghenies makes sense, as Americans have always been more at home with the blind bard than the English have been, this advocate for regicide who doesn't seamlessly integrate with the conservatism of the British establishment. Read by New England Puritans as the great advocate of religious nonconformism, feted by the American revolutionaries as a prophet of liberty, and taught for centuries from Harvard to Suffolk County Community College, Philips Andover to the Bronx High School of Science, as an exemplar of learning and composition. Today, however, though Milton is still a shibboleth of the educated, I'd venture to say that his name is more widely known than are his words, a figure more admired than actually read. As Erik Gray writes in an essay from *The Los Angeles Review of Books*, "What Milton lacks, unlike Shakespeare, is fans."

Count me on Team Milton. Shakespeare is an enigma, a chimera, a ghost—a figure so ambiguous that since the nineteenth-century cranks have been spuriously stating that he didn't write his own works. Milton, on the other hand, could be nobody other than Milton. Incorrigible, grumpy, staid, and—often despite himself—conceited. There is something undeniably human about Milton, even as he soars to levels of brilliant eloquence that by themselves are borderline supernatural. Such language—lush, fecund, rich—undergirds *Paradise Lost*. At times this sort of thing, gorgeous even when it's hard to understand, comes across as mere throwaway line:

> Sweet is the breath of morn, her rising sweet,
> With charm of earliest birds; pleasant the sun
> When first on this delightful land he spreads
> His orient beams on herb, tree, fruit, and flower,
> Glist'ring with dew; fragrant the fertile earth
> After soft showers; and sweet the coming on
> Of grateful ev'ning mild; then silent night
> With this her solemn bird and this fair moon,
> And these the gems of heaven, her starry train:
> But neither breath of morn when she ascends
> With charm of earliest birds, nor rising sun
> On this delightful land, nor herb, fruit, flower,
> Glist'ring with dew, nor fragrance after showers,
> Nor grateful ev'ning mild, nor silent night
> With this her solemn bird, nor walk by moon
> Or glittering starlight, without thee is sweet.

Shakespeare, as befits a relative commoner born in the sixteenth century, has a biography of lacunae. Milton, by contrast, has reams written about him; there is certainty about where he was (mostly), what he thought (the majority of the time), and what others felt about him (all of the time). Son of a moneylender with pretensions to music, Milton grew up on Bread Street in Cheapside at the center of Stuart London, educated in Greek and Latin at St. Paul's School and later trained at Christ's College, Cambridge. His father was a devout Protestant, his grandfather a Catholic recusant, all generations of the Milton family inheritors of the contentious settlements of religion that marked the Reformation. Milton penned his first major poem "On the Morning of Christ's Nativity" in 1629, a retelling of the Christmas story from the perspective of the pagan gods who were defeated in the birth of the messiah, a precursor to the syncretism which would define his most famous work a half-century latter. In 1630 he'd be included in a reprinting of Shakespeare's folio, Milton's contribution a dedicatory sonnet to his celebrated predecessor, the "Dear son of memory, great heir of fame." His earliest poetic heights were perhaps reached with "Lycidas" in 1637, less than a decade after his graduation from Cambridge and written in honor of a student named Edward King who drowned in the Irish Sea, an unfortunate young man whom biographers have argued provided the poet more of an opportunity to wax eloquent than to have necessarily felt any deep genuine affection toward, the celebration of he who "knew / Himself to sing, and build the lofty rhyme" more for the author than the pastoral elegy's subject.

Drawn to poetry over the ministry, Milton strategically planned out the course of his career, adherent of the classical model of authorship which understood any writer as having to naturally progress through certain levels of difficulty as pertains genre, culminating in epic as the apotheosis of what literature could do—a schedule which he precisely followed. His earliest verse was deeply enmeshed in subjects classical, even borderline pagan, as with his masque *Comus*, performed in 1634 for the master of Ludlow Castle, where "Before the starry threshold of Jove's Court/My mansion is." Despite his reputation for Puritanism, Milton was always a poet of dueling antipathies, the resolute Protestant who supped with Jesuits, the doctrinaire Christian who harbored heresies in his breast, the mystic drawn to sensual physicality and the bureaucrat who promoted regicide. An English nationalist, he nonetheless adored the continent, particularly Italy, where he traveled from 1638 to the following year, finding an opportunity to meet the aged and blind Galileo under house arrest (an auspicious event that he'd make much of) before returning to a homeland on the verge of revolution. During those years of civil war, as the High Church Royalist Cavaliers of King Charles I fought the largely Puritan Parliamentarian Roundheads (so-called because of their common haircut), Milton would become an adept pamphleteer in the latter cause, advocating for any number of radical political programs, nothing more so than justifying the eventual execution of the monarch. Such loyalty was well-compensated as Milton ascended to the position of Secretary of Foreign Tongues in the Commonwealth government of Lord Protector Oliver Cromwell. For eleven years it was Milton's responsibility to translate official documents into Latin, a de facto diplomat between the revolutionary government and the other European states, his mastery of the lingua franca an aid in the international politics as the poet was already so well-respected. Also a perilous position to be in when King Charles II returned at the invitation of Parliament in 1660 after Cromwell's death. The younger Charles, not partial to those who advocated for his father's decapitation, put a warrant out for the arrest and execution of Milton, who went into hiding, but was eventually pardoned due to the intercession of his more chameleon-like ingratiating colleagues such as poet Andrew Marvell.

Through political defeat and the increasing darkness of glaucoma, Milton propelled himself into that Parnassian realm of eternal bards that he'd long coveted to be included besides. In shockingly quick succession, Milton's final decade was spent polishing *Paradise Regained*—about Christ's temptation in the desert—and *Samson Agonistes*—a closet drama intended not for performance but only to be read—both of which were printed in 1671. Broken but unbroken, fallen but redeemed, blind but he could see. This was less the passing of Milton's historical moment, even as all of Interregnum advocacy came to naught, than it was his passing into eternity as he began to write from a perspective almost atemporal. "But he, though blind of sight," Milton wrote of the biblical hero Samson, though obviously with somebody closer in mind, "Despised, and thought extinguished quite,/With inward eyes illuminated,/His fiery virtue roused/From under ashes into sudden flame." Drawing from scripture and myth, apocrypha and occultism, linguistics and even physics, Milton was the last of the Renaissance men, the final individual who with his propensity to language and learning could stake claim to knowing everything which it was possible to know, before specialization and disciplinary division cordoned us off into our own lonely library silos. Finished three years before he would die, *Paradise Regained* was the culmination of Milton's religious introspections, and yet for all the poem's brilliance, it's difficult to be similarly engaged with "Victory and triumph to the son of God" as readers are to *Paradise Lost*. That epic—printed in 1667 and finished in the Satanic year before—has nothing which compares to it, not even by Milton. No other book encompasses the maximalist perspective which Milton was somehow able to conjure, ranging from Copernican physics to Lapland witches, New World discoveries to the nature of the Trinity. The author, or narrator, or what-have-you, is somehow a character within it. The reader is somehow a character within it. Since first reading Milton's words in McIlvaine, I've been honored to write about Lucifer for *The Atlantic* and the poem's physics for *Aeon*, Milton's sense of time for *Poetry* and his demons for *The Paris Review*, and I must confess that after all these years I'm still not sure that I'm any wiser than I was then that cold February day when between the listing for the great Margaret Cavendish and the anthology's appendix, I first discovered *Paradise Lost*.

Book III—Narrative

Thee Father first they sung Omnipotent,
Immutable, Immortal, Infinite,
Eternal King; thee Author of all being,
Fountain of Light, they self invisible
Amidst the glorious brightness where thou sit'st
Thron'd inaccessible.

—*Paradise Lost*, Book III

on forever's very now we stand.

—e. e. cummings, *50 Poems*

Wearing a navy-blue suit that looked like Saville Row but was most likely purchased from one of the Jewish tailors along Fifth Avenue in the Hill ("Dress British, Think Yiddish"), Albert Labriola's demeanor didn't connote the stodginess, tweediness, or dowdiness which we might associate with the phrase "Milton scholar." Not only a Milton scholar, but one of the great Milton scholars—an astute, perceptive, brilliant Milton scholar. I only ever heard Labriola speak a few times, first at an event welcoming a new cohort of adjunct composition instructors to Duquesne University where he was the Dean of the McAnulty College and Graduate School of Liberal Arts, that brutalist campus perched upon a bluff overlooking the Monongahela River and adjacent to Downtown Pittsburgh. The professor was a familiar presence during my first-year teaching at the school, a debonair gentleman who (and I might be misremembering this) seemed as if he always had a fresh flower in his lapel. Labriola died from a heart attack in 2009, just a year after I started working at Duquesne, the culmination of interrelated illnesses he'd been suffering from for several years. The passing of one of the giants of twentieth-century criticism, with Michael Lieb writing in *Milton Quarterly* that "Al was certainly one of the most 'humane' humanists of his generation . . . truly a *Mensch.*"

Like me, Labriola was a native Pittsburgher. Also like me, he was Italian-American. Unlike me, Labriola was a powerhouse scholar who brought visual arts to bear on interpreting English Renaissance literature, editor of the *Variorum Commentary* on Milton, founder of the Medieval and Renaissance Literary Studies Series at Duquesne University Press, author of dozens of scholarly papers with imposing titles like "The Aesthetics of Self-Diminution: Christian Iconography in *Paradise Lost*," as well as editor of the journal *Milton Studies* for two decades, not to mention the recipient of six service medals, including a Bronze Star, earned in Vietnam. For both of us, however, something in *Paradise Lost* was enrapturing, with Labriola writing in the journal *Modern Philology* that "beyond human creativity . . . Milton looks to the primal Creation and the pristine state of humankind . . . a prophetic poet contemplating the potential of what humankind may create artistically, scientifically, and politically, including the very poems on which he himself is at work." A son of Bloomfield, that neighborhood of aluminum-sided row houses and concrete stoops going down the infinite line of Liberty Avenue toward Downtown, tomato plants grown in window sills and statues of the Virgin Mary or St. Francis in the small side lawns some are fortunate enough to have. Along with Constantinos Patrides who was Greek, or Stanley Fish who is Jewish, Labriola brought an ethnic perspective into that WASPy citadel of seventeenth-century English literature, an assault on the ivy-covered-ivory-towers. As Labriola's sartorial decisions evidence, that involved a *je ne sais quoi*. Class. Style. Humor. A way of cutting through the dross. Which brings me to an event held by the Biology Department in honor of Charles Darwin's two hundredth birthday at which Labriola was to say a few words. Asking the assembled what the one book was which the great naturalist took with him aboard the HMS Beagle, an intrepid undergraduate guessed that it was the Bible. Labriola feigned being aghast and said, "Not the Bible! Darwin had with him a vast improvement on the source material! Milton's *Paradise Lost!*"

I'm not sure that *Paradise Lost* is a vast improvement on the entirety of the Bible, that cacophonous library of Bronze Age texts by hundreds of scribes. Would I trade *Ecclesiastes, Job,* or *Song of Songs* for Milton? I'm not sure. For sure I would be willing to hand over *Leviticus* or the *Epistle to the Romans* for *Paradise Lost*. Yet at its core, Labriola was correct that Milton's epic wasn't just a commentary, wasn't just inspired by the Bible, but that Milton intended to produce his own prophecies. After reading *Paradise Lost*, the Bible is not the same; after Milton wrote his poem, neither the

Hebrew Scriptures nor the New Testament remain exactly as they had been before. Like a wayward planet wandering through the solar system, Milton's poem irrevocably altered the orbits of all those other planets that had been there long before. Such is the nature of *Paradise Lost*'s gravitational pull. Thinking, reflecting, writing about Eden's apple or the thrashing of the serpentine demons in Hell in our post-Milton epoch is different. Only Dante's *The Divine Comedy* is equal in reconceiving what exactly scripture means, and as he created Catholicism through his tripartite journeys into perdition, purgatory, and paradise, so did Milton radically revise the Protestant perspective. Like all brilliant apocrypha, from the *Book of Enoch* to the *Gospel of Thomas*, Milton expanded outward, envisioning new stories from short passages, putting flesh onto the bones of scripture as with those skeletons in Ezekiel.

The plot is from Genesis, the first book of the Hebrew Scriptures, as well as from Revelation, the last book of the New Testament. Adam and Eve's temptation in the garden, the war in heaven and the subsequent fall from Heaven, all of it here. Describing Milton's radical pamphleteering during the civil wars, and Nicholas MacDowell observes in *Poet of Revolution: The Making of John Milton* that he mastered a "kind of counterintuitive reading of the Bible, in which passages are made to yield a meaning and validate an argument which is apparently the opposite of what they seem to say," a method that "will become characteristic of

Milton's treatment of scripture." *Paradise Lost* need not be read against the grain to find its subversive core, because its author has already done that for us (perhaps of the Devil's party). He has added texture, detail, and depth; conversations among the archangels and the Lord, discourse between God and Christ (who are discrete from one another), a new cosmology in which the universe is created from Chaos. None of this is incidental; Northrop Frye writing in *The Great Code: The Bible and Literature* argues that Milton "understood that changes in metaphor were far more important than changes in doctrine." Perhaps this was unconscious or implicit, but Frye is correct that poetry precedes theology, stories exist before faith. In rewriting scripture in soaring, beautiful, transcendent language, Milton wasn't merely justifying the ways of God to man, he was also justifying the ways of man to God. An act of inspired creation, one which courted heresy, but that took faith more seriously than apologetics ever could. Whether Milton was bragging in his declaration that *Paradise Lost* was written to accomplish something without precedent is irrelevant; the fact that he achieved it is what's remarkable.

The great twentieth-century German-Jewish Marxist literary critic and unrepentant mystic Walter Benjamin wrote in his essay "On the Image of Proust" that "it has rightly been said that all great works of literature establish a genre or dissolve one;" how self-evidently correct is that observation of *Paradise Lost?* While reading Homer's *The*

Iliad and Virgil's *The Aeneid* at St. Paul's, Edmund Spenser's *The Faerie Queene* at Cambridge, and Ludovico Ariosto's *Orlando Furioso* and Torquato Tasso's *Jerusalem Delivered* while in Tuscany, Milton aspired to write an epic which surpassed them—and he did. Homer may have sung of one man's "twists and turns/driven time and again off course, once he had plundered/the hallowed heights of Troy," but Milton's lyre vibrated to the creation of the universe. Virgil had "sang of arms and a man,"but Milton's was about Heaven and Hell. Ariosto's epic clanged with the battles of "knights, of passions and of wars, / or courtliness, and of valiant deed" while Tasso noted that "For God and country, all things are allowed," but Milton's purposes were greater than nation, greater than even the Lord, for his epic was about reality itself. What gives *Paradise Lost* its infinite power is that where Homer, Virgil, Ariosto, and Tasso relish the clashes of men, Milton's War in Heaven is where existence itself first cracked. Even stranger, the more significant scene is two people simple eating an apple. That's the power of the poem, for what's fused is the sacred and the profane, the miraculous and quotidian, heaven and earth.

Epics have traditionally told of the foundation of great empires, be they Homer's Greece, Virgil's Rome, Spenser's mythic Britannia. Milton concerns himself with the universe. What Milton understands is that the most significant acts can be the ones which are most mundane. While the Bible threads through literature, the "Great Code" of which Frye speaks (drawing the metaphor from Blake), its language, themes, and stories are replete through Western culture, nobody had every quite done what Milton did. Anglo-Saxon rewritings of creation and Medieval morality plays about the crucifixion are one thing; an epic exploration of our prelapsarian world is quite another. During Milton's schooldays, epic was the poetic achievement most worthy of laurels; neither lyric, nor drama, nor prose could compete with the sustained, versified narrative that took the affairs of great men and the founding of nations as its subject. Spenser was Milton's nearest contemporary and model, a wicked man who advocated for ethnic cleansing during the sixteenth-century colonization of Ireland and whose unfinished epic *The Faerie Queene* was intended to be for Queen Elizabeth what *The Aeneid* was for Caesar Augustus. The author of *The Faerie Queene* prayed that "Fierce wars and faithful loves shall memorialize my song," but Spenser's most dedicated reader surpassed him in almost every way.

That earlier epic is brilliant in its own way, unwieldy and inchoate as it sometimes is, with its panoply of allegorical characters and Arthuriana (interestingly enough a young Milton's favored subject for a future epic was nothing less than Camelot), but compared to *Paradise Lost* it reads as Medieval. Which is another curious thing about Milton, for as archaic as he superficially seems, he is a poet more out of time than simply of the past, in keeping with the quality of great literature that acts as a singularity, both devouring all that which came before while making it impossible for future light to fully escape. If Benjamin's claim is correct, and I think it is, then it's telling that following Milton no great epics were ever penned. There are admirable attempts, everything from Joel Barlow's idiosyncratic *The Columbiad* in the eighteenth-century to Stephen Vincent Benet's twentieth-century Civil War epic *John Brown's Body,* but at its core Milton buried the most significant genre in literary history (while making way for the ascendancy of the novel). And as a singularity, *Paradise Lost*'s greatness exemplifies nothing as prosaic as mere canonical significance. Rather Milton was able to somehow pen an epic which existed beyond past, present, and future, where the characters weren't just Achilles and Ajax, Aeneas and Dido, but God and Satan—and far more importantly, both you and me.

Across ten "books," each prefaced with a prose prologue stating its central argument, later restructured into twelve books with the 1672 edition, and over ten thousand lines and a little under eighty thousand words, *Paradise Lost* did nothing less than rewrite the world itself. Narratively organized in a manner that's prefigures cinema, Milton jump-cuts between two major plots: the reconstitution of the rebel angels after their expulsion and the first couple's time in Eden leading up to their own exile. *Paradise Lost* begins *in media res,* the disorganized, discombobulated, and disordered fallen angels awakening in the sulfury, fetid, stinking environs following their defeat. Reassembled, the demons begin what's effectively a political debate. What is to be done as regards their loss? Where is their next stand against the divine order to happen? How shall they govern in perdition? "Better to reign in Hell, than to serve in Heaven" is the consensus, as they construct their parliament of Pandemonium (a Latin neologism for "All Demons"). That bon mot is often offered in favor of the argument that *Paradise Lost* has something a bit Luciferian about it, or is at least sympathetic to its most famous character. As byzantine as Milton's poetry can sometimes be, that Lucifer gets all the best lines (and the poet could, if anything, turn a phrase when he wanted to) is evidenced for the Puritan's (unconscious) infernal allegiances. Maybe. It's something that's worth considering at greater length, but needless to say the "Milton problem" has been a scholarly preoccupation across four centuries—why did a Christian poet craft such an evocative, beguiling, fascinating, attractive character as Satan? Why did he invent a new way of talking about the Devil as rebel, revolutionary, romantic hero?

A variety of other characters are introduced throughout the first two books, demons and pagan gods whom Milton drew from his prodigious knowledge of religion and mythology. Mammon, the demon of avarice and prodigious hoarding of wealth; Beelzebub, the Lord of Flies; Mulciber, the soot-covered deity of industry; and Moloch, blood-besmeared Carthaginian deity of child sacrifice, to name only a few. Squabbling between themselves, the Pandemonium debates the proper way in which to enact revenge against the God who has defeated them in battle. Having existed in a time before time, with past, present, and future mere shadows, it was during their fall that God created Earth—created Paradise—which Satan proposes he will corrupt by tempting the first couple, fully adult, though still in their infancy. In this way, Satan and his followers intend to once again launch an assault against nature, reality, and God, "For who can yet believe, though after loss, / That all these puissant legions, whose exile / Hath emptied Heaven, shall fail to re-ascend, / Self-raised, and repossess their native seat?" This conspiracy of Moloch, Beelzebub, and Satan will tempt this human couple—designed in perfection, enthroned in paradise, and yet lesser than the celestial beings who once encircled the throne of God, radiating holy hosannas for all eternity—and corrupt them with sin, an infection that will forever define all generations henceforward.

God doesn't appear until Book III and tellingly the Lord lacks any of what makes Satan evocative. Where Satan is impassioned, eloquent, attractive—where Satan is *sexy*—God is an unctuous, boring prig. The Lord watches as Satan makes his way through Chaos toward Eden, for "Long is the way / And hard, that out of Hell leads up to Light," espying the Devil's reverse harrowing with His "offspring of heav'n born." Christ, not yet incarnated as Jesus and known variously as the "great Vice-regent," "King Messiah," and simply "Son of God" is not coequal to his Father, one of the many heresies Milton countenances. Christ is wholly more sympathetic than his Father, though not without his martial abilities, having been the celestial being that reigned triumphantly against the rebel angels during their war. As for the Father and Son's viewing of Satan's journey through the black ether of Chaos, God reveals that he's fully aware that Adam and Eve will be tempted, but denies any responsibility, explaining that "I made him just and right, / Sufficient to have stood, though free to fall," a clever if hypocritical bit of theological square circling. With a movie director's innate sense of editing, Milton shifts the action away from the golden spheres of Heaven back to Satan's ascent, the Prince of Lies bemoaning "which way shall I fly / Infinite wrath and infinite despair? / Which way I fly is hell; myself am hell." Satan comes to Eden disguised as a bird, and having overheard the divine prohibition against their eating from the Tree of Knowledge of Good and Evil, he transforms into a toad and whispers temptations into the sleeping Eve's ear.

The middle portion of *Paradise Lost*, wedged between two epic falls, constitutes that which for many readers is the most lagging part of the poem, though Books V through VIII are replete with turns of phrase, observations, and philosophical profundities. These four books are dominated by discourse between the Archangel Raphael and Adam on the nature of creation and the universe, with the former recounting the drama of the War in Heaven, the Creation of the world (as performed by the Son, not the Father), then culminating in an unusual scientific lecture about the Ptolemaic and Copernican models of the solar system, an issue of no small accounting in seventeenth-century England. This section grapples with the scientific and philosophical questions which revolutionized the early modern West, and tellingly Milton is agnostic about issues such as if the solar system is geocentric or heliocentric, an agnosticism that masks a willingness to flout orthodoxy. His knowledge concerning "centric and eccentric scribbled o'er, / Cycle and epicycle, orb in orb" when it came to mathematically describing the rotation and revolution of the planets speaks to Milton's familiarity with the new physics, in his pride at having met Galileo during his Italian sojourns. Galileo himself appears in *Paradise Lost*, his discovery of sunspots discussed in Book III, and toward the beginning of the epic itself he is referred to as the "Tuscan artist." This strange inclusion is crucial to how time works in the poem, for though ostensibly taking place at the beginning of Creation, the eternity which existed before Eden and which still endures in Heaven means that there are no boundaries before past, present, and future. The same reason why the narrator—the author—the poet—is a character within his own poem, as we all are present in *Paradise Lost*.

The crescendo—Eve's temptation—awaits the ninth book. "Her rash hand in evil hour / Forth reaching to the fruit, she plucked, she eat: / Earth felt the wound, and Nature from her seat, / Sighing through all her works, gave signs of woe / That all was lost." To swallow perchance to fall. Eve's eating of the forbidden fruit is freely chosen, but she has been unwittingly influenced by Satan (finally disguised as the Serpent, "subtlest beast of all the field"), and is unaware of the full implications of her transgression. Tellingly, though he is aware of the cost, Adam joins his wife in this violation out of a sense of loyalty, the closest which *Paradise Lost* has to a tragic hero. Milton's depictions of their relationship belies a tenderness he lacked in his own life; he was married three times, with his first marriage to Mary Powell particularly unhappy and leading the pamphleteer to advocate for divorce, an unconventional position at the time (to say the least). That's not even to begin to conjecture on Milton's potentially conflicted sexuality, from the snark about his effeminacy to the passionate writing he devoted to his childhood friend Christopher Diodati. Yet in *Paradise Lost* the first couple are a model of marriage, enjoying conjugal relations even in Eden. More than that, Milton extols tenderness, intimacy, love. It's a strange experience of reading the sentimental Milton with what we know of his biography, his politics, his reputation, and yet Eve's pre-expulsion meditation on her husband that "So dear I love him, that with him all deaths / I could endure, without him live no life" is all the more moving because of the stern and doctrinaire man we envision writing those words. What makes their exile such a tragedy is that before it's a cosmic disruption, it's a domestic one. Had the fall not happened, Eve and Adam would inhabit paradise for an innocent eternity, but as it was, that experiment was doomed to failure, and the result is this corrupted world. And all of us.

In Book X the Son arrives to pass judgment on them while also interceding in mercy, the two allowed to live on earth for the period of their natural lives, even though the bliss of immortality is denied them and their progeny. Sin and Death, the incestuous product of Satan's cursed loins, arrive to hold dominion over creation. Returning to Hell in triumph, Satan and his assembled demons discover that God has transformed them into a hideous brood of hissing vipers, the once beautiful form of Lucifer reduced into this bestial, reptilian, monstrous cacophony, thus drawing the most enigmatic and evocative character of *Paradise Lost*'s narrative arc to a close with a "dismal universal hiss, the sound/Of public scorn." The final two books aren't without drama; Book XI features the Archangel Michael presenting a tutorial to the couple on the history of the world up through the great flood of Genesis, while alluding to the incarnation of the Son. Most movingly is the conclusion of *Paradise Lost*, as that woman and man designed in perfection and intended for paradise are compelled to make their long road out and east of Eden:

> Some natural tears they dropp'd, but wip'd them soon;
> Their world was all before them, where to choose
> Their place of rest, and Providence their guide:
> They hand in hand with wand'ring steps and slow

Through Eden took their solitary way.

What is so profound—so moving—so beautiful—about Milton's concluding lines are how he is has transformed something mythological into an intimate account of the human condition which is nonetheless universal, and how he has converted the inert skeleton of scripture into something pulsing with feeling, with novelistic energy. Whether or not Al Labriola was correct that Milton's epic is superior to the Bible, it's clear that *Paradise Lost* can't be reduced to scripture. No other epic poem has done what Milton does in these last lines; the Bible doesn't do what Milton did in these last lines. He has made the first couple *human*. Furthermore, he has expressed something axiomatic about our lives, the "solitary way" in which we must make our path in the world, born alone, dreaming alone, dying alone, while also promising that through the abyss and in the darkness, there is still the possibility of confronting that gapping maw, that dark void, while walking "hand in hand." What all the millions of words about *Paradise Lost* so often occlude is that Milton's poem is a love story.

Book IV—Inspiration

Descend from Heav'n *Urania*, by that name
If rightly thou art call'd, whose Voice divine
Following, above th' *Olympian* Hill I soar,
Above the flight of *Pegasean* wing.

—*Paradise Lost*, Book VII

The duende's arrival always means a radical change
in forms. It brings to old planes unknown feelings
of freshness, with the quality of something newly
created, like a miracle, and it produces an almost
religious enthusiasm.

—Federica Garcia Lorca,
Theory and Play of the Duende

For ten uncharacteristically cool weeks in the summer of 2014, I lived in that haven of ivy-covered Tudor homes and granite-stoned cottages, red-brick apartment buildings and low modernist ranch houses that is flat, rectilinear Hyde Park. My residence was a dorm that had been built only five years before on the wrong side of the Midway Plaisance, where once the luminescent but disposable dreamlike monuments of the 1892 World's Fair had stood, now the home of dense Gothic university buildings, all dark stone and gargoyle. Enrolled in National Endowment for the Humanities seminar, my afternoons were spent in discussions about the seventeenth-century metaphysical poet George Herbert's influence on America's greatest poet Emily Dickinson. We scanned for meter and rhythm and close read for metaphor and allusion, but as with all things poetical something intangible and ineffable was in play, what Herbert called "those delights on high," or how Dickinson wrote of a "Vastness . . . A Wisdom, without Face, or Name." Questions of, as they both knew well, *inspiration*. At night I'd go to the Woodlawn Tap on E. Fifty-fifth Street, once the favored watering hole of Saul Bellow, who if not known as a prodigious drinker at least had a taste for the dingy environs of a great dive bar (more characteristically, back when it was still Jimmy's Bar, Dylan Thomas is said to have stopped there). Goose Island after Goose Island, kept down with one or two of their disturbingly cheap cheeseburgers, and then I'd stumble back south. In the morning, awoken by Rockefeller Cathedral's heavy bells, I'd startle forward while facing the clean wall of my dorm so that when my eyes opened, with the blinding light of a Chicago July permeating my entire field of vision, all I could see was that simultaneously oppressive and liberating whiteness in all of its nothingness and infinity. I'd almost always assume that I was already dead. A vision of what's to come.

During the days that weren't occupied with arguing about the status of Transubstantiation in Herbert's *The Temple* or Spiritualist allusions in Dickinson, I'd wander Powell's and the Seminary Co-Op looking for cheap paperbacks gifted by the families of long-dead professors, I'd sit at Promontory Point following the horizon's slight curvature of the earth from the towers of Chicago to the smokestacks of distant Gary, chilled in the early evening from Lake Michigan's breeze rolling across what used to be prairie, and often I'd explore the heavy-wooded interior of the Oriental Institute, where you can examine baked clay steles with wedge-shaped Akkadian cuneiform speaking of the heroes of Uruk, or you can see gold-foil coated status of that Canaanite mountain deity El, whom the Hebrews borrowed a name from for their own lonely God. By coincidence, the El was also what Chicagoans called the spray-paint decorated trains that ran throughout the city and connected the high rises of the Loop to the heavily guarded island of Hyde Park amid the blighted South. Within that thick-necked, broad-shouldered, obstinate hog-butcher-to-the-world of America's third city, there are few locations that I find more immaculate than the Art Institute of Chicago. Guarded by bronze lions on Michigan Avenue as the museum abuts Grant Park, cocooned from the cacophony of concrete and glass, the clattering of train over the shadow of platform, symphony of jackhammer and car horn. One of those greatest-hits kind of museums, which isn't a knock on their collection, far from it. Walking through halls of marble and granite and steel and glass the visitor is at risk of "Art Attack," of being surrounded by so much stimuli that it can be difficult to fully comprehend the space you're in. For some this is related to simply seeing so many famous paintings and sculptures in such close proximity. For others, it's simply the sheer preponderance of images, facing the mortal finitude of being a single human. And for many, it's a religious experience, a sense of the transcendent in seeing such technique, dedication, and, most of all, inspiration.

George Seurat's massive *A Sunday Afternoon on the Island of La Grande Jatte,* with its pointillist picnickers by the Seine, a painting which feels like sunlight on a spring day. Edward Hopper's *Nighthawks,* so iconic that it borders on cliché, a couple and a solitary man sitting at the counter in an all-night diner in Greenwich Village, the stark greens and reds illuminated in faint glow, a painting which feels like loneliness in the early morning. Pablo Picasso's melancholic *The Blue Guitarist,* an elderly man, more joint and bone than flesh, fingering the fret of his instrument, his head down, his face mournful, his eyes absent, a painting that feels like the dark origin of inspiration itself, a quality which the great Spanish playwright Federica Garcia Lorca could have described as "duende." Lorca named the quality of pathos that animates the most mysterious of received inspirations after the mischievous sprite, wicked home-spirits, hobgoblins, and elves of Spanish folklore; now the title had been repurposed into a term for the melancholic muse of the most genuine of art. Lorca saw the duende as manifested in forms like flamenco and the bull fight, yet duende itself, he admitted, is ecumenical. Art and literature can't be entirely tamed, codified, explained, or translated into pure algorithm. Duende—inspiration—grace. All are mysterious, they are never deserved but they can never be denied, for literature and art are wholly more glorious and much more blessedly dangerous. Just down the hall from those duende-haunted compositions at the museum, not far from Seurat or works by Cezanne, Monet, Degas, and Van Gogh (all manifesting Lorca's spirit), there is a composition made by the Swiss artist Henry Fuseli in 1793 that for what it lacks in fame it makes up for in representing the moment of inspiration, a work entitled *Milton Dictating to His Daughter*.

Purpled and corpuscular, Milton sits on the far right; his countenance is grayish but his hands are pale, while his face's grim complexion and his upturned glowing eyes seem possessed. He stares heavenward, focused on something which only the blind poet can see; Fuseli's Milton is enraptured, in a painful ecstasy, in a deep trance. In the middle of the painting one of Milton's daughters stands contrapasso at a podium, engrossed in copying her father's recitations with quill pen onto a sheaf of papers. Just as the poet is lost in a poetic reverie, light seems to radiate from her. To the far left, behind the other two, another daughter is busy doing needlework, feminine drudgery to contrast the amanuensis' role, or to maybe compare to it. A supernaturalism permeates Fuseli's work, the dark Milton and his bright daughter portrayed in a Manichean interdependence, the origin of inspiration difficult to ascertain. Milton with his possessed eyes calling on an infernal muse, his daughter with her radiance a collaborator in *Paradise Lost*, at the very least because the words of her father must be written in her handwriting. The scene is borderline surreal. Fuseli often returned to Milton, in keeping with the Romantic era's obsession with the poet, painting an entire series about the poet's work, making the artist the most significant visual interpreter of *Paradise Lost* between his late eighteenth-century contemporary Blake and the French engraver Gustave Doré some five decades later.

A lithe Eve emerging from Adam as watched by a a hazy neoclassical God appearing more Olympus than Sinai and rendered in chiaroscuro hues; a heroic and perfectly proportioned Satan as if Hercules twisted back in pain while Sin emerges from his brow; the first woman, still nude in her prelapsarian innocence, leaning against the prohibited tree while lured by the serpent, a chimera whose human face is of Eve herself, sinful temptation mirroring our desires. Fuseli even painted brief references from *Paradise Lost.* When in Book II Milton compares the hell hounds who accompany Sin to the "night-hag . . . riding through the air . . . Lured with the smell of infant blood, to dance / With Lapland witches, while the laboring moon Eclipses at their charms," an enigmatic allusion to the indigenous pagan people of Scandinavia and their reputation for being Hecate-worshiping witches, Fuseli painted a bare-chested, blonde hag staring skyward while she holds a baby upon an altar, a scene which doesn't appear in the poem other than as that quoted sidebar. He does the same thing with another passage, one where Milton compares the fallen angels to fairies "Whose midnight revels by a forest side

. . . On their mirth and dance/Intent, with jocund music charm . . . At once with joy and fear his heart rebounds"— painting a circle of beautiful sprites wheeling in the sky over the sleeping head of a troubled shepherd.

In *Milton Dictating to His Daughter*, there's no muse or angel twirling in the heavens above the poet, yet the color and light, expression and position, indicates that Fuseli sees divine inspiration at play. This is not something Fuseli invented, mind you; there's a long tradition of understanding *Paradise Lost* as divinely inspired, notably beginning with Milton himself(he says as much in the poem). *Muse* is a word that in contemporary parlance has shifted from its original meaning. Today, it refers to anybody who inspires a writer, or artist, or director, but for the ancient Greeks a muse was a supernatural entity, a goddess who imparted poetic genius. Greek poets disagreed on the exact number, but nine has become the standard over the past two-and-a-half millennia. Categorized by their particular domain, individual muses could intercede for certain genres; Euterpe for music, Terpsichore for dance, Urania for astronomy, Clio for history, Thalia for the pastoral, Melpomene for tragedy, Erato for lyric, Polyhymnia for sacred poetry, and Calliope for the epic. Tracing the ways in which belief in the muse draws upon trance, intoxication, and the ecstasy reflected in primeval shamanistic practices, E. R. Dodd writes in *The Greeks and the Irrational* how "all achievements which are not wholly dependent on the human will, [such as] poetic creation contains an element which is not 'chosen,' but 'given.'" A divinely inspired madness, whereby the muses could be invoked in eruptions of genius.

As old as verse itself. "Sing to me of the man, Muse, the man of twists and turns / driven time and again off course," says Homer in Robert Fagles' translation of *The Odyssey*. "O Muse! the causes and crimes relate; / What goddess was provok'd, and whence her hate; / For what offense the Queen of Heav'n began / To persecute so brave, so just a man," intones Virgil in John Dryden's rendering of *The Aeneid*. By the Middle Ages and the Renaissance, authors as varied as Dante, Chaucer, and Shakespeare all employed such language. Invoking the muse became more rhetorical conceit than ritualistic formula; a way of connecting yourself to tradition. With Milton, there is the sense that on some level he believes in the reality of this muse in a way that Chaucer, Shakespeare, and even Dante didn't. "Sing Heav'nly Muse, that on the secret top / Of Oreb, or of Sinai, didst inspire / That Shepherd, who first taught the chosen Seed, / In the Beginning how the Heav'ns and Earth / Rose out of Chaos," Milton writes in Book I, connecting himself to the scribes of Genesis, connecting literary creation to the weaving of reality itself. Both bring order out of disorder, the former imposes on narratives, ideas, and characters an elegant wholeness. "Invoke thy aid to my adventurous Song, / That with no middle flight intents to soar Above th' Aonian Mount," he declares, and then Milton does. Book VII is where he names his "celestial patroness," and she is not Calliope, but rather incongruously Urania, associated with astronomy. Why not call upon the muse of epic, why not ask for the intercession of any of the other poetic spirits, be they Clio, Thalia, Melpomene, Erato, or Polyhymnia? Because Milton is not writing mere history with its dull recitation of events, *Paradise Lost* dwells in Eden but it is not boring pastoral, it is a tragedy beyond all other tragedies, and the sacred verse of Polyhymnia isn't even commensurate. Calliope's epic scope can't encompass *Paradise Lost*, for Milton sings not of the arms and man and Greece and Troy but of the *Universe*. And so no muse other than Urania could be called upon. Milton is the last poet to call upon the muse who may have actually believed in her. He is the last poet where we almost believe him ourselves.

Milton had planned to write an epic since his youth, when he sketched out ideas for an Arthurian poem which he never wrote, but while there is debate about the exact schedule of *Paradise Lost*'s composition, consensus is that the writing itself began after Charles's restoration to the throne, when the poet was a hunted (if ultimately pardoned) man. Destitute, discredited, and defeated, Milton was also blind by this point, so that the logographic poet who'd scribbled so many millions of words was unable to do so by the time he was ready for his opus. Royalist detractors saw in his glaucoma punishment for his vociferous defense of regicide, while Milton himself made connection between his disability and the trope of the blind bard. A new Tiresias. "Milton's belief that *Paradise Lost* was divinely inspired has embarrassed some critics," writes John Carrey in an essay for the *Times Literary Supplement*, but it's a "claim made unequivocally in the poem itself." So singular is the epic, that sometimes what's forgotten is how bizarre the actual writing of it was. When Milton attempted to write during the day, the wells of Parnassus were dry. But upon sleep, the blank verse of *Paradise Lost* flowed into him as if from without, Milton actually hearing the voice within his unconscious mind. Upon awaking, Milton commandeered the assistance of his family—normally one of his daughters with his first wife Mary Powell—in transcribing his reveries. There would be some editing—Carry tells us that around half of the lines would be shortened or cut entirely, so that there is both "an official poem, articulating ideas that are endorsed by Milton's conscious intention, and there is an unofficial poem, releasing disruptive meanings that Milton would not have consciously endorsed," calling *Paradise Lost* the only "poem of considerable length . . . composed while the author was asleep." Lest we assume that this is just a conceit within the poem itself, both his third wife and daughters would confirm that *Paradise Lost* was written in a manner similar to how Fuseli imagined it, the poet in the gloaming of morning repeating what Urania had delivered.

Of the poet's five children, only the three daughters of his first wife Mary Powell survived into adulthood: Anne,

Mary, and Deborah. By the time *Paradise Lost* was being set for the printer, Anne was twenty, Mary was eighteen, and Deborah was fifteen. It's believed that Mary and Deborah were those who acted as scribes, his oldest daughter dismissed by Milton's earliest biographers as having been mentally delayed. His youngest daughters were enlisted in reading aloud to him in Latin, Hebrew, Italian, and Greek, languages which they lacked fluency in, while mornings involved endless copying. Today we'd rightly describe much of this as abusive. Nor was their relationship with his third wife without complications (to put it mildly); Dr. Johnson records that upon Milton's marriage to Elizabeth Mynshull, Mary said "that was no news to hear of his wedding but if she hear of his death that was something," while the critic also records that the poet's widow "oppressed his children in their lifetime, and cheated them at his death." Most egregiously, Milton personally educated his nephews John and Edward Phillips (the latter a great translator in his own right), but didn't see his daughters worthy of tutelage, even while they were handmaidens to the language's greatest poem. Mary and Deborah Milton were the epic's unheralded scribes, and perhaps its collaborators. Tradition has so long emphasized the sui generis nature of Milton's inspiration, and yet it stretches credulity to assume that Mary never corrected a comma, or that Deborah never altered a semicolon. Writing, as anyone who has ever had an editor knows, is collaborative. This does nothing to diminish inspiration, rather it spreads it outward democratically. Carry writes that it's "hard to say how he imagined his muse. But it is clear that he thought she was female, presumably because she spoke in a woman's voice, and very close to God." Is it so hard to believe that Mary and Deborah's voices became intermingled with Urania's, so that Milton could scarcely tell them apart?

What makes the transcription so remarkable is that it's a demonstration of possession, a record of the transubstantiation whereby oral literature is made flesh (or paper, as it is). *Paradise Lost* is performance and product, it is both the writing and that which is written. The poem is the evidence of the muse's inspiration after everything else has been burnt away. *Paradise Lost* was first uttered like *The Iliad* or *The Odyssey*, no different from *Gilgamesh* or *Beowulf*, or any other spoken epic, yet it was instantly crystallized into a permanence. Comparison of the "foul papers" of uncorrected drafts and the "fair papers" of final versions demonstrates that Milton didn't revise or edit much. What's remarkable is that an epic of such intricate complexity, such perfectly structured prosody, is basically a first draft simply amended here or there and that it was *first spoken out loud*. Devout Muslims often count one of the many miracles of Allah being the perfection of the Qur'an, the Archangel Gabriel reciting it exactly to the Prophet Muhammad. Similarly, the voice is so close to perfection that *Paradise Lost* could be considered a record of Urania's veracity. The words, the lines, the books, the sheer immensity of the work's composition itself, the artistry of its creation is inextricable from the end result. As it should be, for any work dealing with the idea of creation must mimic a bit of what's sacred about that process. George Steiner writes in *Grammars of Creation* that such an "analogue between divine and mortal acts of creation was, in the fullest sense, theological." Reading *Paradise Lost* through the God forg'd manacles of enchantment and it is the last of the truly inspired works, the final prophecy, the concluding scripture.

What then of Urania? Was she real? It's the wrong question, because of course she was, had the muse not been whispering into Milton's ear like the Serpent into Eve's, we'd have no poem. In a more literal sense, her existence is an illusion, a day dream, a bit of Milton's unconscious. Edward Hirsch writes in *The Demon and the Angel: Searching for the Source of Artistic Inspiration* that "what these poets are describing is transcendence of the ego, a sense of merging with the whole. The alien force that dwells within us—a demonic inspiration—is experienced as a 'death' to the ego, which has been forced to yield the psyche to a nonrational power that has captured it." What's resurrected from the ashes of the ego is the poem written while truly enraptured, in the midst of a river with currents much stronger than you can swim against. Anyone captured by that flow has felt it, whether a poet crafting their lines, a playwright spinning dialogue, an author lost in their own plot and unsure of what will happen next, yet arriving at their destination anyhow. Call this motivating power what you will—unconsciousness—inspiration—muse—inner light—duende—but it's something that can neither be reduced to the neurotransmitters or cultural forces. Literary theory and criticism are painfully and stupidly allergic to mysticism, and yet *Paradise Lost* is the great rejoinder to those empirical reductionisms which attempt to exorcise the poem of any of its transcendence, grandeur, or mystery. That *Paradise Lost* exists is as great a work of art as any single line within *Paradise Lost*. It is the remainder of inspiration after the self has been divided, an artifact of something supernatural (as all honest writing is). *Paradise Lost* compels us to face just how metaphysical, just how supernatural, literature actually is. What it offers is an experience more Orphic, more hermetic, more occult than that which can be imagined, where poems arrive wholesale from muses and the words which you utter are never quite your own. An inspiration of such intense glory that it's as dark as infinity and as bright as nothing, like our existence bleached to the most immaculate and beautiful void.

Book V—Words

Through utter and through middle darkness borne
With other notes then to th' *Orphean* Lyre
I sung of *Chaos* and *Eternal Night*,
Taught by the heav'nly Muse to venture down
The dark descent, and up to reascend.

—*Paradise Lost*, Book III

Thus a poetical word is a thing conceived in itself
and includes all its meanings.

—William Empson, *Seven Types of Ambiguity*

If the seventeenth-century antiquary John Aubrey is to be believed, then in 1673 the Poet Laurette John Dryden called on Milton during the last year of the latter's life to request his blessing in preparing a stage adaptation of *Paradise Lost* that was to be titled *The State of Innocence* and in which the distinctive blank verse of the original would be "corrected" to more pleasing rhyme. "Dreyden Esq. Poet Laurete, who very much admires him, & went to him to have leave to putt his Paradise-lost into a Drama in Rhyme," writes Aubrey in his 1681 complication *Brief Lives.* An arresting scene— the first official Poet Laurette in Caroline resplendence, all powder, velvet, heel, silk, fur, and feather, meeting with the dying Puritan to ask for permission to tar his greatest poetic masterpiece. Where Milton was a republican, Dryden was a royalist; the author of *Paradise Lost* was a low church Protestant, while the future author of *The Hind and the Panther* would one day convert to Catholicism; the former had been a member of the Interregnum government that closed the theaters, the latter would become the greatest playwright of the Restoration stage. Even more complicated, for Dryden had also worked with the Commonwealth, wrote *Heroic Stanzas* in honor of Cromwell, and had acted as a pallbearer to the Lord Protector at his 1658 funeral, along with Marvell and Milton himself. By 1660, with Charles on the throne, and Dryden would write *Astraea Redux* celebrating Restoration, with Marvell discovering similar royalist positions. The two of them were good at surviving, Milton wasn't. He was lucky, however, and had powerful friends who were fond of him.

Dryden's visit was a tremendous honor; the esteem in which the Poet Laurette held Milton wasn't feigned. Between the two, readers far preferred Dryden. Rather than dour meditations on original sin, Dryden invented romantic comedy with his play *Marriage a la Mode;* instead of stern denunciations of the crown, he penned patriotic verse like *Annus Mirabilis*; rather than theological contemplations about the nature of the Triune God, the Poet Laurette wrote the satirical *Mac Flecknoe* and *Absalom and Ahithophel.* In keeping with the radical innovations of staging, costume, and casting (including allowing actresses), Dryden was the unparalleled master of the theater, a writer of spectacle. His plays *The Indian Queene* and *The Indian Emperor* retold the story of Cortés and the Aztec King Montezuma, with serious historical liberties, while using actual Indian artifacts, including a hammock and colorful feathered headdress brought back from Suriname by the novelist Aphra Behn. With bombast and explosion, he staged the Spanish *Reconquista* of Islamic Iberia in his play *Almanzor and Almahide, or the Conquest of Granada by the Spaniards.* Dryden even refashioned Shakespeare's *The Tempest*— for a generation his was the standard. What he did with Shakespeare, he hoped to do with Milton, making the thudding blank verse of *Paradise Lost* palatable to an audience that couldn't abide its lack of rhyme. If there is any element of prosody for which Dryden is remembered, it's this—the grandiose, lyrical, and most of all suspiciously *poetic* rhyme scheme of the heroic couplet. Every line's end rhymed with the following line's end, so that Dryden modeled how verse would be written through the Restoration and almost the entirety of the eighteenth century. Today Dryden seems stilted, affected, self-conscious, and bluntly a little goofy with all those rhyming couplets. He sounds like a jingle writer. Regardless, and not without reason, even if he's more of his own time than all time, Dryden was still a poet of genius—there's no Alexander Pope without Dryden's heroic couplet, no Phyllis Wheatley either.

Dryden's verse does exactly what people expect poetry to do—it rhymes. And it rhymes *obviously.* "What flocks of critics hover here to-day, / As vultures wait on armies for their prey, / All gaping for the carcass of a play!" Milton, by contrast, didn't rhyme—that's what blank verse is, unrhymed iambic pentameter. Though drama had abandoned rhyme as far back as 1561 with Thomas Norton and Thomas Sackville's play *Gorboduc,* exemplified with Marlowe's naturalistic "mighty line" and having its consummation with the works of Shakespeare, epic still demanded the Italianate finery of rhyme. Until *Paradise Lost.* Milton's most avant-garde innovation, and while many understood its genius—including Dryden—many found it rough, uncouth, and lacking beauty. By contrast, Dryden *aggressively* rhymed, which is why he was Poet Laurette and Milton wasn't (the regicide also had something to do with that). And now Dryden comes to Milton's death bed with a suggestion to "correct" *Paradise Lost,* to keep its plot but to justify the ways of God to man in heroic couplets, and to stage it for the entertainment and edification of the theatergoer. "Mr. Milton received him civilly," Aubrey reports, "& told him he would give him leave to tagge his Verses." Not just a generosity, but a condescension, for the dying Milton was confident enough in his own genius that he didn't see Dryden's gauche and gilded "tagging" as doing much to subtract from his own genius. And he was right.

The State of Innocence was spectacularly popular; the most reprinted of Dryden's dramatic works. Where Milton's epic was experimental and difficult, Dryden's libretto "fixed" all of the byzantine syntax, the baroque diction, the unconventional grammar, the confusing punctuation. A valedictory poem by Nathanial Lee included in a 1677 printing gushes that Milton did "rudely cast what you could well dispose:/He roughly drew . . . A Chaos, for no perfect World was found,/Till through the heap, your mighty Genius shined." Lee's obsequious brown-nosing is embarrassing. All the more so, because despite Dryden's admitted literary accomplishments, *The State of Innocence* is objectively bad. Gone is all the thunder and triumph of Satan's rhetoric, subtracted is the gentle poignancy of Adam and Eve's love, or the stunning erudition that meanders through those complex, enjambed, blank verse sentences. Gone is the oracular sublimity of "The mind is its own place, and in itself/Can make a Heav'n of Hell, a Hell of Heav'n," replaced with Lucifer saying "These regions and this realm my wars have got;/This mournful empire is the loser's lot;/In liquid burnings, or on dry to dwell/Is all the sad variety of hell." Suddenly Satan sounds less like a romantic hero and more like a rap battle's loser. When it comes to prosody— when it comes to diction, syntax, grammar, punctuation— the actual words on the page matter far more than mere narrative. This is disagreeable to post-moderns for whom synopsis can replace reading, but I'll affirm this, for here I stand and I can do no other—words themselves and how you choose to arrange them take primacy over the story. Plenty of genres tell stories, and do it well—songs, film, everyday conversation. But to be great literature, it all begins and ends with the quality of words and the arrangement the author puts them in. If the words are perfect, then it doesn't matter what tale is being told.

Because Milton was a revolutionary, in all the ways that matter, there was a lack of appreciation for *Paradise Lost* during his life. Even his old friend, defender, and occasional transcriber Marvell wrote that *Paradise Lost* would have been more agreeable had Milton only seen fit to use "tinkling Rhyme." Not that people didn't acknowledge his learning—they did. And not that they didn't find him a genius—he was considered such. But the epic was unconventional, eccentric, idiosyncratic. His decision to reject rhyming was confusing, controversial. Always the patriotic Englishmen, Milton understood rhyme as unnatural in his native tongue, the imposition of French prosody onto his language. He's not entirely wrong; romance languages are rich in words that end with vowels, making rhyme a natural element of verse written in French, Italian, Spanish, and so on. English, by contrast, is a staccato and guttural language, and prior to the eleventh-century Norman conquest, English poetry was devoid of rhyme, rather structuring itself around alliteration which comes far more naturally. With his blank verse, Milton hoped to liberate the "Heroic Poem from the troublesome and modern bondage of Rhyming." According to the poet, rhyme itself is "trivial," arguing that in English a "True musical delight consists only in apt number, fit quantity of syllables, and the sense variously drawn from one verse to another." A benefit to blank verse is that in cadence, rhythm, and intonation it's the meter which sounds closest to everyday speech. Shakespeare may have a reputation for difficulty because of the vagaries of early modern English, but if you compare the celebrated soliloquy in *Hamlet* to the rhymed language in the thirteenth-century anonymous *Everyman,* the former sounds much closer to how people actually talk. Beer argues that the similarity to Marlowe and Shakespeare wasn't incidental, that "Milton's choice suggests . . . his vision of epic as a kind of drama . . . perhaps a nostalgia." Every day we naturally slip into blank verse, we transition into a rough iambic pentameter with its alternating rhythm of unstressed and stressed syllables, the plodding "de DUM, de DUM, de DUM" which is perfect for the rough and angular sounds of English. We never accidentally slip into long stretches of rhymed language.

Such cadence gives *Paradise Lost* the sound of conversation, but that exists in stasis with Milton's labyrinthine syntax and baroque diction. Despite the seeming patriotism of rejecting rhyme, Milton relishes the Latinate, that language being the first in which he wrote verse. Additionally, the epic is a complex web of allusions—to mythology, scripture, canonical literature, and apocryphal religious writings, all of which Milton availed himself of in their original tongue (fluent in as many as twelve languages, including a reading familiarity with the Ethiopian tongue Ge'ez). Coming upon this nest of seeming confusion, many readers dismiss Milton as a show-off, the star student bragging about all which he has studied, but this complexity and erudition serves a purpose, with Michael Schmidt arguing in *The Lives of the Poets* that " Latinate syntax and diction allow flexibility and through echo or etymology create complex harmonies inaccessible in a simpler style." What Milton conjures then is not mere meaning, but an over-abundant, supersaturated, explosion of meaning. So much meaning that *Paradise Lost* becomes a universe. If we're to consider his brilliance in terms of theme, subject, and narrative, then we must first understand his transcendence in prosody. That means taking due consideration of the words on the page, for poetry is incantation. The poet W.H. Auden, no fan of Milton's politics, still argued that he was "the first to make a myth out of his own personal experience, and to invent a language of his own remote from the spoken word." Milton was a magician, an alchemist, an enchanter, a conjurer, and *Paradise Lost* is his spell.

Paradise Lost is so dense with allusion that Milton can sometimes seem a bit too difficult. Schmidt explains that "If you grapple with his marvelously complex language, you lose sight of its place within his elaborate and allusive forms; if you try to characterize his politics, you find the texture of the verse often running against the structure, as though his imagination was correcting what his partisan mind wanted to say." Ambiguity, paradox, metaphor, allusion, formalism— all of these are qualities which the early twentieth-century New Critics valorized, seeing in poetry the opportunity to construct ingenious mechanisms that could be objectively plumbed, and in close reading the chance to demonstrate their interpretive acumen. Such a methodology lends itself to poets who excel at wordplay and complexity; both Donne and Herbert came back into scholarly vogue precisely because of the New Critics. Any of Donne's immaculate *Holy Sonnets* can generate rewarding close readings—and they did. Writing thousands of words about a fourteen-line poem by Donne is one thing, but trying to understand the ten thousand lines of *Paradise Lost* in its entirety is another. Of the New Critics, only William Empson produced a sustained reading of Milton, though it was brilliant (and to be discussed latter).

Cutting, carving, splicing, and slicing *Paradise Lost* can only get the critic so far; it'd be like performing an autopsy on Picasso to find cubism's origins, or Einstein to better understand general relativity. Still, there are clearly certain appraisals which can be made of Milton's verse, and the scalpel of close reading is estimably useful in analyzing individual portions. Consider lines 910 to 919 from Book II:

Into this wilde Abyss,
The Womb of nature and perhaps her Grave,
Of neither Sea, nor Shore, nor Air, nor Fire,
But all these in thir pregnant causes mixt
Confus'dly, and which thus must ever fight,
Unless th' Almight Maker them ordain
His dark materials to create more Worlds,

Into this wilde Abyss the warie fiend
Stood on the brink of Hell and look'd a while,
Pondering his voyage.

"Reading lines like this is almost a physical labor," writes Terry Eagleton in *How to Read Poetry*, "as the eye struggles to unravel the intricate syntax and negotiate a path through the bristling thicket." Eagleton argues that blank verse becomes crucial in these passages, since rhyme would be more pleasing to the ear, but perhaps in that easiness obscure something about he words themselves. As it is, the unrhymed iambic pentameter "slows us down, forcing us to experience the celebrated Miltonic music in all its high-pitched rhetorical bravura." Milton has two purposes here; the first to present the scene where Satan stands on the coast of Chaos, considering his next moves from Hell toward Eden. The second is to explicate a cosmology of creation, a model for how existence arises from Chaos. Amazingly, he achieves this dual purpose in only one sentence!

Concerning the poet's first purpose, the passage is tense with incipient drama, certain phrases announce themselves—"wilde abyss," "His dark materials," "warie fiend," and "Stood on the brink of Hell." Satan having "Stood on the brink of Hell" isn't about entering that place, but leaving it. Surprising, if not paradoxical, a way in which to contrast Hell—which despite its horrors is still a place of meaning created by God—and Chaos which is formless, meaningless, a void, an abyss. Chaos is the singular aspect of Milton's metaphysics, and here he gestures toward its complex relationship to God and creation. Abandoning the doctrine of ex nihilo creation, Milton explains that this prior realm is both "Womb of nature and perhaps her Grave." That Milton chose that final word rather than the obvious "Tomb" underscores both his rejection of rhyme and his abandonment of a clichéd trope. His choice of "perhaps" is interesting, for if creation emerges out of Chaos there's no certainty that it shall absolutely return to it. A contingent apocalypse. In the third line, he gives litany of Chaos' constituent substances, emphasizing that none are discrete, but forever intermingled. Milton makes expert use of rhetorical anaphora, underscored with those monosyllabic words—"Of . . . Sea, nor Shore, nor Air, nor Fire." These are the classical elements of Greek cosmology, with Milton simply using the word "Sea" for "Water" and "Shore" for "earth." He preserves the alliterative pair that start the line, as well as an assonance with the final. That the elements have their "pregnant causes" speaks to Chaos' primordial nature. It may be a void, it may be terrifying, but it's also from whence existence arises. Order first necessitates disorder.

Creation didn't abolish Chaos, to the contrary that latter state perennially exists at the margins of reality. All of those elements in Chaos which "must ever fight" in an inchoate scrum maintain themselves in that disorganization "Unless th' Almighty Maker them ordain/His dark materials to create more Worlds." Consider what Milton is arguing here—that God is capable of creating "more Worlds"—note that plural. Without elaboration, Milton has suggested that God is capable—if he hasn't already—of creating other universes, parallel realities. Suddenly the difference between literal and mythic truth is put into stark contraposition. Milton is unclear if these other creations are real or not—"Unless" indicates a lack of knowledge on that score—but it's obvious that such an act is possible. Then there are the fascinating "dark materials" which are the Lord's provenance, the adjective an inversion of qualities we normally associate with God, an allusion to Isaiah 45:7—"I form the light and create darkness: I make peace and create evil: I the Lord do all these things." Finally, we have this romantic image of brooding Satan standing on the "brink of Hell" (with that final word both a place and a prediction), where he is "Pondering." Such a fantastic word, with its connotations of introspection, meditation, analysis. When listing attributes of Satan, an affinity for pondering is surprising, and yet that particular word adds to the sense of the character as capable of cold, ruthless calculation, of a methodical rigor that differentiates him from the bestial representations of the Devil from the Middle Ages.

"Each sentence, every image, every word, has a number of functions to perform on literal and moral levels," writes Schmidt. Such is the promise of all language which aspires to literature, as opposed to merely communicative words. The New Critics merely secularized a method which had undergirded the interpretation of sacred scripture for millennia. Call it hermeneutics or exegesis, but it's an expectation that poetry gestures beyond itself, not that it's a straightforward code that only need be cracked. The most sublime of verse has hidden within it passages, ornamentations, mirrors, secrets, deities known and unknown. Language exists to communicate simple messages, but when it's self-referential, it becomes literature. Poetry is when language thinks about itself. What Milton did with *Paradise Lost* is to craft new scripture with endless meanings precisely at the historical juncture when his fellow Protestants precluded complexity and allegory within the Bible. The result is a poem of "enormous scope in space," as Schmidt writes, which "incorporates eternity." So straightforward is the process of close reading—you just read something closely, right?—that I don't think I really appreciated its utility well into graduate school. What I've learned is that a brilliant close reading is able to tell you something about a work of literature that you wouldn't have noticed on your own. For such a close reading to be possible, however, a work of literature must have certain qualities of richness, power, significance, and enchantment already implicit within, otherwise you're no longer interpreting something, you're reading into it. Virtually anything can be close read, but how rewarding that experience will be depends on the work. That which we think of as the "best which has been thought and said," as Victorian critic Matthew Arnold described it in *Culture and Anarchy,* the "sweetness and the light," which has that quality of sublimity, or beauty, or truth that engenders close reading.

But some works—some very few and very rare—seem to do something more, they seem infinitely interpretable, they have whole universes hidden within. Dante's *The Divine Comedy*. Herman Melville's *Moby-Dick*. Walt Whitman's *Leaves of Grass*. James Joyce's *Ulysses*. Possible to misread all of these works—I certainly have. There are, as always, good and bad interpretations, valid and invalid readings. What marks them, however, is this theurgical quality of it being impossible to exhaust all readings. Ever since I first flipped through *Paradise Lost*, I've found it so pregnant with meaning that it's dizzying, exhausting to read. Milton is painful, not because he's dry or boring, but because each sentence, each line, each word seems to direct one toward some endless multiplicity of meanings. It's saturated with significance. A poem which demands that you catch your breath, where reading can make you feel as Satan must have felt as he fell through Chaos. What I affirm is that to write poetry is to incantate and to craft narrative is to conjure, and that to combine the two is to be the greatest of occultists. All brilliant writers are such magicians, but by this standard, Milton is an alchemist of the rarest variety. Joyce quipped that if Dublin were destroyed, it would be possible to rebuild the city based entirely on *Ulysses*. I'd venture that after the apocalypse, God would be able to recreate the universe using only *Paradise Lost*.

Book VI—Satan

His form had yet not lost
All her original brightness, no appear'd
Less than archangel ruin'd, and th' excess
Of glory obscur'd.

—*Paradise Lost,* Book I

You pronounced your words as if you refuse to
acknowledge the existence of either shadows or
evil. But would you kindly ponder this question:
What would your good do if evil didn't exist, and
what would the earth look like if all the shadows
disappeared? After all, shadows are cast by things
and people.

—Mikhail Bulgakov, *The Master and Margarita*

The second greatest fictional character in all of literature is God in the Bible; the greatest of all literary protagonists is Satan in *Paradise Lost*. Like many a macabre reader, especially us lapsed Catholics, I think that I'm a little obsessed with Satan. I've written about Satan, I've taught courses about the Devil, I've published a book on demonology. When I was a teenager, I'd play the Rolling Stones's "Sympathy for the Devil" on repeat. Charlie Watts's drum syncopation—Keith Richards's fiendish guitar solo. Even better was "Paint It, Black," which if not literally about Lucifer still sounded more Satanic. Rock music wasn't all that I'd boom before my parents got home, absentmindedly strutting through the house with visions of demons in my head. Carl Orff's grandiose *Carmina Burana*, especially once you move beyond the cliché of "O Fortuna," still evokes a Satanic coven whenever I hear it. If I do have a fixation on the Prince of Darkness, I should say that its not in a goth way, nor am I some occultist adhering to a mélange of Friedrich Nietzsche and Ayn Rand. Still, the Devil gets all the good tunes. I'm fascinated by Satan because he's evocative, charismatic, sexy, rebellious, and dangerous, and like a lot of you I can't help but pay attention when Lucifer is on stage. More to the point, that Satan is evocative, charismatic, sexy, rebellious, and dangerous has little to do with scripture, and everything to do with Milton.

As rendered by theology and by Milton, God is not a fascinating character. Omnipotent, omniscient, omnipresent, omnibenevolent, He is also inert, vacant, and insipid. Water or air are as engaging a personality; one might as well configure reality as a character as much as God. Being depthless, He has no depth; being infinite, He contains no particularity; being eternal, He has no humanity. But in scripture, by comparison, God is a literary triumph. Ancient literature doesn't tend to have fully fleshed protagonists, the bards of antiquity were content with symbols, ciphers, and allegories more than human beings. Homer, or whomever we've elected to call that name, crafted immaculate verse expressing the immediacy of human experience and emotion, but his characters are one-dimensional. Achilles is brave but flawed, Ulysses dogged and courageous, Penelope steadfast and loyal. Though there are exceptions, the writings of the ancient Greeks rendered characters as unchanging as the masks of the Athenian stage, as eternal as the God of theology. Nowhere in Homer are there characters as complicated, contradictory, and human as Hamlet, Emma Woodhouse, Anna Karenina, Clarissa Dalloway, Leopold Bloom. For the poets of ancient Greece and Rome, verisimilitude of personality wasn't their purpose. By contrast, something unprecedented happened in the Hebrew Scriptures.

Erich Auerbach explained in his monumental and magisterial mid-century study *Mimesis: The Representation of Reality in Western Literature* that characters like Abraham, Moses, and God project psychological complexity in a way that ancient Greek characters didn't. According to Auerbach, ancient Jewish literature countenanced the multilayered and the contradictory, depicting a "problematic psychological situation . . . [that] is impossible for any of the Homeric heroes, whose destiny is clearly defined and who wake every morning as if it were the first day of their lives: their emotions, though strong, are simple and find expression instantly." The characters of the Hebrew Scriptures are much more realistic—faithful Sarah laughing at the absurdity of God, the loving father and husband Abraham who is capable of sacrificing his son and cheating on his wife, Jacob who steals his brother's birth-right and becomes the patriarch of a great nation. None of these characters, however, is as much of a triumph as God. The Lord is a brilliant artist who creates the universe from nothing, yet He is seemingly unaware of the first couple's transgressions; a loving Father and a jealous, wrathful deity; an entity lonely in His infinite powers, a singularity without friends. On Olympus, the worshipper pretty much knows what they're going to get from Zeus, Apollo, or Athena, the entire pantheon of those gods; on Sinai, the solitary Lord is much more fickle, capricious, multidimensional.

The God of the Hebrew Scriptures is the first literary character with an inner life. The reasons for this are accidental, for "God" in the Hebrew Scriptures God is an amalgamation of by several different authors of several different characters (sometimes called Yahweh, sometimes named El) who were merged together for political and religious expediency. God is a Lord of redaction. Jack Miles explains that his titular subject in *God: A Biography* is a character whose "inner contradictions" were the "result of the fusion [that] took shape, quite early on . . . it was the biblical writers' common intellectual grasp of this nest of contradictions . . . that permitted them, working over centuries, to contribute to the drawing of a single character." As a result, He's the first conscious character in all of literature, or at the very least the earliest accurate depiction of what the inner life of consciousness looks like. Miles writes that God is "an amalgam of several personalities in one character," but isn't that all of us, with our triumphs and foibles, our loves and hates? We're all much more similar to the God of the Jews than the one-dimensional gods of the Greeks. No fictional character of such antiquity is as glorious in that regard, for if some deity did create humanity, we reciprocated with this triumph fortuitously crafted by accident, a God in our own image. Scripture's God is the second greatest character because it's the first accurate representation of consciousness; Satan is the greatest because he takes the prison of consciousness to its terrifying conclusion.

Satan is first referred to with the definite article in the biblical book of Job. *Ha-Shaitan* in Hebrew translates to "The Adversary," a cryptic quasi-divine being who challenges God to that text's infamous bet. Numerous malevolent spirits and evil demons may have been adversaries previously, but in Job they finally have their chief, albeit the author is short on detail. Earlier references, such as the Serpent in Genesis, aren't actually identified with Satan in the biblical text itself, such interpretations simply being traditions that developed later on. In the New Testament Satan takes on a bit more texture and backstory, such as when he tempts Christ during his forty-day vigil in the desert, or the various references to him in the apocalyptic book of Revelation. As both Judaism and Christianity developed, Satan became associated with ultimate evil. Revelation, drawing from apocryphal Jewish writings, gave account of not just apocalypse, but of the War in Heaven which preceded creation itself. "And there was war in heaven," reads Revelation 12:7, " And the great dragon was cast out, that old serpent, called the Devil, and Satan, which deceiveth the whole world: he was cast out into the earth, and the angels were cast out with him" (note that in *Paradise Lost* it is the Son, and not the Archangel Michael, responsible for defeating Satan in the war). As

Christianity developed, the Archangel Lucifer became not just a manifestation of absolute evil, but a traitor against harmony, balance, and order, a being who challenged God's authority and suffered expulsion into Hell because of it, while degenerating into the reptilian, chthonic, and caprine Satan.

Prior to Milton, Satan was either a figure of fear or a figure of fun. During the Middle Ages, many representations of Satan emphasized his bestial, monstrous, otherworldly qualities, and his evil was all-consuming, inexplicable, absolute. In *The Divine Comedy*, Dante describes Satan as having "three faces: one in front bloodred;/ and then another two that, just above/ the midpoint of each shoulder, joined the first:/ and at the crown, all three were reattached." This Satan is a massive beast forever masticating the crushed bodies of those arch-rebels Brutus, Casius, and Judas, all of them encased in ice. Nothing charismatic about Dante's Satan, nothing attractive—he is horrific, disturbing, cursed. Nobody would want to be Dante's Satan. By contrast, European folk culture, ranging from carnival performances to morality plays, may have offered a less catatonic Satan, yet a creature no more charismatic than the frozen devil in Dante. In Medieval stage performance, Satan was a squawking, farting idiot, easily tricked by Christ during the harrowing of Hell, a creature as fit for laughter as he is for fear, what Jeffrey Burton Russell described in *Lucifer: The Devil in the Middle Ages* as a "trivial and comic demon." With *Paradise*

Lost, Milton has rejected both the animalistic monstrosity of Dante and the comic devil of the Medieval stage, crafting rather a visionary, magnetic, beautiful triumph whose angelic origins are obvious, and whose attractive and compelling rhetoric, personality, and appearance underscores a far more terrifying lesson about evil. Having fallen to Hell, this Satan declares "Here at least/We shall be free; the Almighty hath not built/Here for his envy, will not drive us hence:/Here we may reign secure, and in my choice/to reign is worth ambition though in Hell." Now this—*this is a Satan who you might want to be.*

Revelation is sparing in Satan's reasons for raising of a third of the angels against Heaven, but exegetical interpretations have developed over the centuries. The first-century apocryphal text *The Life of Adam and Eve* claims that Satan and his followers refused to bow down to the newly created first couple (note the different chronology here), and were thus punished for their intransigence. In the Qur'an, the Islamic equivalent of Satan, who is known as Iblis, refuses to bow before Adam and Eve because only God is worthy of worship, making the Devil the most faithful of monotheists. In *Paradise Lost*, God demands that Satan prostrate himself before the newly created Son, a plot point that's neither scriptural nor orthodox, but which acts as Milton's explanation for the War in Heaven. Beyond the immediate reasons for rebellion, Milton's God is a petty and arbitrary tyrant, His demands hew less to reason than

His own capricious dictates, and Satan's rebellion can't help but seem estimably justified, as his soaring rhetoric would indicate. Nothing spoken by God is ever the rhetorical equivalent of Satan, and so Milton crafts an entirely new type of character, far richer and more complicated than the mere cipher offered by scripture and tradition. Russell notes in *Mephistopheles: The Devil in the Modern World* that many readers saw in Milton's Satan a "determination to be true to himself, enduring every defeat and agony in his fierce adherence to his own identity in the face of a superior power determined to destroy him."

Paradise Lost's Satan isn't just a rebel, he's a rebel against an unjust cosmic order; he's a revolutionary against the relativist faith which holds that good and evil are only what God defines them as. Medieval Scholastic philosophy described God as being circumscribed by certain laws; as Aquinas argued, not even the omnipotent deity can make a triangle have four sides—or make good evil and evil good. In some ways the Reformation, particularly in its Calvinist forms, elevated God by chaining humanity, for at the exact historical juncture that belief in free will became anathema to many Protestants, the Lord's liberty was made absolute, four-sided triangles and all. Empson, in his classic critical work *Milton's God*, sees the deity of *Paradise Lost* as a monstrous authoritarian, comparing him to Joseph Stalin and slurring the Protestant God as the "wickedest thing yet invented by the black heart of man." In this reading, Satan is the poem's unequivocal hero, a revolutionary who wages war against what Milton called the "tyranny of Heaven." Indeed, one doesn't need to read Calvin's *Institutes of the Christian Religion* to see a monstrous God, as that second greatest fictional character in all of literature is already pretty monstrous within the Bible itself. This God who drowns the entire world and who demands that Abraham sacrifice his son so as to prove his faith, the Lord that compels genocide and who murders first-born sons.

Besides, any belief in an omnipotent and omnibenevolent God must answer for the ancient question of theodicy, of how such a being could allow evil in this world, could tolerate the suffering of the innocent. That is the central question of Job, that most radical work of scripture, which depicts God's judgment as capricious and arbitrary, and His justifications as irrelevant and unconvincing. With more than a bit of atheistic pluck, Empson writes that "if some bully said he would burn me alive unless I pretended to believe he had created me, I hope I would have enough honor to tell him that the evidence did not seem to me decisive," concluding that "I dare not despise Satan for making this answer." Evil is enough to condemn the Lord Himself and to throw your lot in with the supposed Prince of Darkness. Satan appears the hero of *Paradise Lost* because God seems so awful, and in the former's declaration of "But what if better counsels might erect our minds and teach us to cast off this yoke? Will ye submit your necks and choose to bend the supple knee?" there is a revolutionary ultimatum, a declaration of independence. Satan is the greatest character in literature because he wages war not just against kings and magistrates (as Milton himself had done), but against "Heaven's awful monarch." What makes Milton's vision sublime is that the reader almost agrees with Lucifer's position. But what make *Paradise Lost* a tragedy is that Satan "begins as a prince of hell and ends as a hissing viper," as Russell writes, when he tries to replace God's arbitrary order with his own relative judgment, for as beguiling as Empson's arguments are, they're also not the only way to understand Lucifer.

Understanding Milton as a partisan of Cain, an ideologue of Judas, an advocate for Satan, has a venerable history, arguably the dominant way of reading *Paradise Lost*. Blake famously remarked in his epic *Milton* that his subject was "of the Devil's party without knowing it." This perspective held that whatever Milton may have claimed regarding his intent, that regardless of his Protestant bona fides, his vision was basically gnostic, that he understood God as a demiurge whom Satan admirably challenged, though the Devil tragically failed in his mission. In an 1807 watercolor set illustrating scenes from *Paradise Lost*, Blake depicts Satan as a muscular, perfectly proportioned, beautiful, blond young man who rouses his demons to action, while in another image Lucifer appears with the serpent coiled around his nude body as he spies on Adam and Eve, and then after the successful temptation soars over

Eden as the angel which he always was, the only sign of his corruption being that his wings are not feathered but chiropteran. John Martin, in an 1823 lithograph with the provocative title of *Eve's Dream—Satan Aroused,* represents the King of Hell in a martial helmet and naked with only a few wisps of tastefully arranged cloth as he brandishes a spear with one hand and a shield with another, a burst of light emanating despite the bat wings folded behind him. The bat wings remain in Gustave Dore's illustration for *Paradise Lost* in 1897, Lucifer with long locks and a Roman military breast-plate leaning against a rocky crag of Hell, one arm thrown over his beautiful face in romantic despair. Indeed, Milton's Satan is a kind of ur-Romantic hero, that archetype defined by Frye in *A Study of English Romanticism* as being "placed outside the structure of civilization . . . yet with a sense of power, and often leadership, that society has impoverished itself by rejecting." Milton's Satan has many faces and many names; he is Captain Ahab in *Moby-Dick* and the titular scientist in Mary Shelley's *Frankenstein,* the alchemist in Goethe's *Faust* and the vampire in Bram Stoker's *Dracula.* Why he remains grander than all of them is that Satan waged war not against a whale, or society, or nature, or even death, but against the Tyrant Himself.

Does Milton mean any of it? That's the big question, the so-called "Milton Problem." Scholars of the poet have had no shortage of fascinating things to investigate—Milton's philosophical materialism, his radical politics, his dissenting religious faith—but finally what most of us come back to is the question of just how much of the Devil's party he was. Blake's contention remains the favored one for many, in part because it's so sexy. Empson took that position to its final extreme, but no shortage of those among the admirable opposition have also claimed that *Paradise Lost* is a conventional Christian poem about the lures of evil and the wickedness of sin, not least of all because Milton says that's what the poem is about. C.S. Lewis makes this argument well in *A Preface to Paradise Lost*, pointing out that for all of the Devil's high rhetoric, he has difficulty justifying his rebellion because "No one had in fact done anything to Satan; he was not hungry, nor over-tasked, nor removed from his place, nor shunned, nor hated—he only thought himself impaired." Satan, in short, is less a revolutionary, according to Lewis, than he is an egoist. The critic doesn't disagree that Satan's poetry is sweeter than those other characters (while making the point that in any work Satan is going to be the most interesting), but that this speaks to Lucifer's narcissism and self-indulgence more than his claimed righteousness. These two positions, between Blake and Lewis, were most memorably squared by Stanley Fish in *Surprised by Sin: The Reader and Paradise Lost* who claims that Milton's poem had a pedagogical purpose, that Satan is so evocative because the poet wants you to think that he's of the Devil's party so that the readers falls for those lies, the better to demonstrate all of our fallen natures.

Hero or villain? Revolutionary or traitor? Liberation or damnation? I've begun to wonder if the character of Satan is a bit like that visual puzzle that sometimes looks like a duck and sometimes like a rabbit. Maybe Milton was neither of the Devil's party or not, and Satan shifts in and out of heroism or villainy depending on which eye is squinting when you read *Paradise Lost*, like a picture that could be a young girl or an old hag, an image that appears as either a vase or two people looking at one another. What I do know is that Milton's anti-hero Satan wasn't just a novel character for all of the reasons I mentioned, but also because his narcissism, egoism, and self-indulgence just as easily elect him as a rugged individualist, a bootstrapper, a frontiersman—an American. That capitalism was made possible by the Reformation is a century-old argument, but perhaps it's not a mistake that Milton's Satan and the free market are the most potent expressions of Protestantism. Satan is cut off from community, tradition, mutual reciprocity, he is rather a solitary man, one who believes himself to be entirely self-made. "In the midst of a world of light and love, of song and feast and dance, he could find nothing to think of more interesting than his own prestige," writes Lewis, and I think to myself, "That would be a clever thing for me to Tweet right now." Satan is a self-promoter—he's on Facebook, and Instagram, and Twitter, and YouTube. "To admire Satan," writes Lewis, "is to give one's vote . . . for a world of lies and propaganda, of wishful thinking, of incessant autobiography." Again, hero or villain? And also again, it depends on which eye is squinting. I do know this—if I'm attracted to Satan against my own best instincts, it's perhaps because the Devil and I are both inhabitants of the United States.

Book VII—Paradise

So on he fares, and to the border comes,
Of Eden, where delicious Paradise,
Now nearer, crowns with her enclosure green,
As with a rural mound, the champain head
Of a steep wilderness.

—*Paradise Lost*, Book IV

This is the most beautiful place on earth. There are
many such places.

—Edward Abbey, *Desert Solitaire*

At the eastern edge of Pittsburgh, only a few blocks from where I grew up, there is an arched stone entrance to the 644 acres of wooded trails, streams, valleys, and craggy overlooks which constitutes Frick Park. Conversion into a public park began in 1931 after the family of the coke magnate Henry Clay Frick—a demonic character himself—donated land for the project. Architect John Russell Pope, the same man who designed the Jefferson Memorial and who had recently finished transforming the Frick family mansion on Fifth Avenue in New York into an art museum, was tasked with constructing the four stone gate houses that act as entrances to the park at various junctures along its perimeter. The gate house closest to where I grew up is off of Reynolds Avenue, in the neighborhood of Point Breeze; it's a tall arched edifice of slate-gray granite with a peaked green ceramic tile mansard roof under which passes a path that then meanders past flat grassland, bocce courts, stone walkways, and another route which leads into the

Homewood Cemetery and then through a forest primeval. No cherubim with flaming swords have to be encountered before passing under the gate. With the park straddling the neighborhoods of Point Breeze, Squirrel Hill, and Regent Square, the Reynolds Street entrance abuts the pleasant, vaguely English-looking stone Tudor homes, brick row houses, and Cape Cods which replaced what essayist Annie Dillard called "The Valley of the Kings," the neighborhood of Gilded Age robber barons like Andrew Carnegie, Andrew Mellon, George Westinghouse, and H.J. Heinz who made this corner of the earth among the wealthiest in the world for a time. Now only Frick's mansion survives, overseeing the northwestern entrance into the park named for him.

To walk through Frick Park—at least for me—is a pilgrimage into Milton's *Paradise Lost,* read not in words, lines, and stanzas, but rather rocks, trees, and water. Descending into the valley you enter an exquisitely maintained illusion of wilderness; a sylvan enclosure not far from the kingdom of traffic noise and bus exhaust, train whistles and sirens. It feels as if you'd returned to seventeenth-century Pennsylvania, when French explorers claimed that a squirrel could jump from tree to tree all the way unto the Pacific. As is the want of some gardens, Frick Park is an exemplary mimesis of nature; pristine, bucolic, and pastoral. The hiker doesn't necessarily notice the sculpted path her feet tread on, blanketed with maple leaves and pine needles, or the irrigation pipes feeding bubbling brooks, and the stone walls shielded by ivy and moss that reinforce hills. Even the strategically placed benches seem more the design of nature than of man. A realm of red oak, green maple, yellow hickory, golden birches, and, as is befitting our fallen world, hemlock. Dogwood, butternut, and even gingko. Squirrels, of course, but also white-tailed deer, some two hundred bird species including owls and wild turkeys, frogs and salamanders, beavers, foxes, badgers, and occasionally black bears that wander in from the actual woods that border the park, those ursine visitors once or twice having ventured onto sleepy early morning city streets. And several varieties of snake—serpents. Regardless of intentional sculpting, Frick Park appears much as it would have in the centuries before coal was mined from Western Pennsylvania hills, before coke was processed and steel produced in mills along the Allegheny, Monongahela, and Ohio rivers. A world before the fall. These are the same woods where during the religious revivals known as the Second Great Awakening a wealthy Massachusetts itinerant farmer named John Chapman, who was an initiate into the mystical Swedenborgian faith, as well as an orchard enthusiast, spread apple seeds on his way into the Ohio Territory, earning his famous nickname. Here is where the Jacobin radicals of the late eighteenth-century Whiskey Rebellion marched, all armed against injustice and inequity with some of them dreaming of a millennial, utopian city descending from heaven onto the Alleghenies and being christened the New Jerusalem. Where a few decades before Scottish General Edward Braddock marched his Virginia regulars—including George Washington and Daniel Boone—from Georgetown, Maryland in an attempt to dislodge the French from the forks of the Ohio while triggering the Seven Years War. He was ambushed not far from Frick Park and his troops were slaughtered, the site now a town which bears his loser's name. Disorder even within paradise. When I die, spread my ashes in Frick Park. It is the most beautiful place I know.

In high school, during a pique of irreverent, profane, blasphemous, sacrilegious, heretical punkery, a friend and I gathered several cheaply bound, orange-covered Gideon Bibles that some evangelists were distributing at my inner-city high school as we left for the day, all of the missionaries the requisite constitutionally mandated distance from public property. With our stack of scripture in hand, we took the bus over to Frick Park, walked beneath the Reynolds Street stone gate house and like Hansel and Gretel left a trail of ripped bible pages along the path, tearing each thin piece of crinkled paper out and letting them fall to the ground like shining white autumnal leaves. Each page shone bright in the orange-fingered sunset of fall's early dusk, squibs of sun even lower beneath the Gothic hooked branches of the tree canopy above, and with every step that led us deeper into the woods, another passage of scripture fell to the earth. *And God said, Let there be light: and there was light—And God said, Let the earth bring forth grass, the herb yielding seed, and the fruit tree yielding fruit after his kind, whose seed is in itself, upon the earth: and it was so—And God created great whales, and every living creature that moveth, which the waters brought forth abundantly, after their kind, and every singed fowl after his kind: and God saw that it was good—And God made the beast of the earth after his kind, and cattle after their kind, and every thing that creepeth upon the earth after his kind: and God saw that it was good—And God said, let us make man in our image.* So he drove out the man; and he placed the east of the garden of Eden Cherubims, and a flaming sword which turned every way, to keep the way of the tree of life. Of my many disobediences.

Follow those paths downward into the base of the park and eventually you'll emerge at the banks of the Monongahela, where across the southern embankment you can view the town of Homestead. A generation ago the mighty smoke stacks of the Carnegie Steel works had forever dyed the sky an ocher glow, millions of tons of molten steel coming off the assembly line every hour of the day, every day of the year, a cacophonous, metallic, empire of industry that with its belching and hammering would have resembled Pandemonium, an evocation of what Milton's great reader Blake described as "those dark Satanic mills," albeit by the nineteenth-century these factories in the United States would have dwarfed anything that the poet had seen only a few decades earlier in southern England. Mulciber's foundry, Moloch's Bessemer converter, and Mammon's bank account on the Monongahela. For a week in 1892, members of the Amalgamated Association of Iron and Steel Workers at the Homestead plant, many of them immigrants, went on strike for better wages and conditions. With Carnegie at his summer home in Scotland, his lieutenant and company operator—Henry Clay Frick—called in agents of the Pinkerton Detective Agency to put down the strike, and in the melee seven of the plant workers were shot and killed, the river running red with blood. What's visible from the banks of the park named for Frick is not the spot where that same man had those workers killed, though seven freestanding smoke stacks still hold sentry in memoriam, but rather the outdoor shopping plaza built upon the ruins of the mill. Should you head east rather than south, you'll eventually come to the town of Braddock, still the site of the Edgar Thompson Steel Works, which even after the collapse of western Pennsylvania's steel industry accounts for more than a quarter of the material produced in the United States. A bit further up the river is the Clairton Coke Works, the largest coke producing facility in the country, which produces so much hydrogen sulfide that its presence alone makes the Pittsburgh metropolitan area the eighth worst for air quality in terms of year-round particle pollution, not unrelated to the region being the third highest for incidents of cancer, with an astounding 20 percent of Pittsburghers ultimately dying from that disease (including my father). East of the park and into the corrupted world, for "Must I thus leave thee, Paradise?—thus leave / Thee, native soil, these happy walks and shades?"

Paradise Lost remains the first and greatest environmental epic ever written. Milton deals directly with issues of industry, ecology, exploitation, and colonization in a manner so seamlessly intrinsic that it's easy to overlook those themes. What Milton's epic is concerned with is the environment of *Paradise* and how through rapacious exploitation it can be *Lost*. Printed a century before even the nascent Industrial Revolution, Milton was still able to draw upon the cannibalistic consumption of the Americas by European colonial powers in imagining what humanity's expulsion from Eden felt like. By the time that the poem was printed, English audiences had been regaled for a century with narratives that described the Americas as perfection, as a place where the climate was temperate, food was abundant, and the people lived in an idyllic state of nature. Thomas Harriot writes in his 1588 treatise *A Brief and True Report of the New Found Land of Virginia* that in America "we found the soil to be fatter; the trees greater and to grow thinner; the ground more firm and deeper mold; more and larger fields; finer grass and as good as ever we saw any in England." In his 1595 report *The Discovery of Guiana*, Walter Raleigh describes South America as a terrestrial paradise, where the Incan Indians repose in a "garden of pleasure in an island ... where they went to recreate themselves, when they would take the air of the sea, which had all kind of garden-herbs, flowers and trees of golden and silver . . . magnificence till then never seen." Two decades later, and the renegade pilgrim Thomas Morton would be even more rapturous in his enthusiasms, writing in his 1622 *The New English Canaan* that "I did not think that in all the known world it could be paralleled for so many goodly groves of trees, dainty fine round rising hillocks, delicate fair plains, sweet crystal fountains, and clear running streams that twine in fine meanders through the meads, making so sweet a murmuring noise to hear as would even lull the senses with a delight sleep." He adds that the "more I looked, the more I liked it."

Such descriptions must have impacted the environmental perspective of *Paradise Lost*, for Milton who read everything had to have read authors like Harriot, Raleigh, and Morton. Keeping with its partial Edenic setting, the epic is replete with lushness and fecundity, the poem taxonomizing subjects botanical, zoological, and geological. Of plants, Milton enumerates the delights of hyacinth, laurel, irises, violets, ivy, pansy, thistle, sedge, myrtle, elm and pines; more exotic plants are also referenced, from the tart citron and delicate red tropical amaranth, to the mighty and holy banyan tree of India, as well of course as the estimably familiar and forbidden "fruit of fairest colours mixt, Ruddie and Gold . . . [for] To satisfie the sharp desire I had Of tasting those Fair Apples, I resolv'd Not to defer." Nor are animals ignored by Milton, as the garden houses sheep and wolves, dogs and lions, as well as bees, doves, bulls, horses, fish, deer, and obviously a serpent (among others). Adam and Eve may have been created with primacy over this world, with the former already intuitively knowing the names of flora and fauna as opposed to being given the responsibility of christening them himself, yet the first couple are also symbiotic with this world, seamlessly integrated into an elysian realm, where their relationship with plants and animals are harmonious, balanced, and ordered. Such claims were often made by European observers like Harriot, Raleigh, and Morton about the native inhabitants of the Americas; that these claims were not just racially condescending but obviously untrue—the boulevards and canals of Tenochtitlan, the sophistication of Incan engineering, and the Mississippi metropolis of Cahokia on the Midwestern plains all attest to the naivety and opportunism of European claims of America's virginal promise—they also were imaginings that configured a different way of doing things, a rejection of the rank pollution and filth even then growing in booming London. Incidentally, the word "American" only appears once in *Paradise Lost*, though that reference in Book IX is a crucial one describing how before the fall the first couple experienced "that first naked glory! Such of late / Columbus found the American, so girt / With feathered cincture; naked else, and wild / Among the trees on isles and woody shores." A fantasy of what life was like among the Algonquin who lived along the Atlantic Coast, or the Iroquois who resided in, among thousands of square miles of other places, what would one day be Frick Park.

A dream of pure ecological sustainability, where even if humanity occupies a higher vantage on the Platonic Great Chain of Being, they're also to be tasked with responsible stewardship. His Puritan coreligionists in New England had largely departed from the previous century's enthusiasms that saw America as a New Eden, rather hearing it as a howling wilderness, and yet this sense of the Western Hemisphere as a place where the fall hadn't happened permeated European intellectual circles, so that a few decades after Milton's epic was published, and the philosopher John Locke could faithfully declare with biblical overtones in his 1689 *Second Treatise of Government* that "in the beginning all the word was America." Privatization, industrialization, and even civilization had infected a *degeneration* about the world that now corrupted these newly found lands. America was a world before the fall, but by the time that Milton was writing that Eden had been assaulted for two centuries by its own demons traveling across the Chaos of the Atlantic to exploit, pillage, and rape. Not that Milton would have been unaware of the shameful record of colonialism, even while like many English he minimized his own kingdom's role in such atrocities. Among stolid Protestants the bloody exploits of the Spanish in the New World were well accounted for in what's known as *El Leyendra Negra,* "The Black Legend," with its tales of blood-thirsty conquistadors and zealous inquisitors. The Dominican friar Bartolomeo de las Casas's 1542 first-person *A Short Account of the Destruction of the Indies* was both accurate and still essential to English propaganda, the tale of despoiling colonists who like Satan introduce evil into Paradise. It was first translated from Spanish into English by Milton's nephew and tutelage John Phillips. A claim that *Paradise Lost* is "really" about colonialism, or industrialization, or the environment is bound to be risible to a certain type of reader who is staid, traditional, conservative. What's risible is the claim that anything as multi-faceted and polyphonic as *Paradise Lost* is "really" about one thing, but certainly Milton's epic is partially about *that* thing. How could it be otherwise, how could a century which saw the despoiling of that which was considered an Eden not be on his mind when writing about how paradise was lost? As J. Martin Evans observes in *Milton's Imperial Epic,* ultimately *Paradise Lost* does happen to literally be about "a corrupt and power hungry adventurer [who] discovers the New World, enslaves its inhabitants, and takes possession of their land."

Whither because of Satan or industry, the fall is experienced through the loss of connection to the natural world, so that "progress" signals a cleaving from the environment which we evolved in, that nurtured us. "O unexpected stroke, worse than of death!" laments Eve in Book XI, and there are few plaintive cries about our exile from nature more melancholic than hers. "O flowers, / That never will in other climate grow, / My early visitation, and my last / At even, which I bred up with tender hand / From the first opening bud, and give ye names!" The horticulturist's mourning, as Eve realizes that the easy climate, the lush foliage, the pliable beasts will all be consigned to memory, as she and her husband must confront a wholly darker, colder, meaner world. "How shall I part, and whither wander down / Into a lower world, to this obscure / And wild? how shall we breathe in other air / Less pure, accustomed to immortal fruits?" Fallen reality is but a pale shadow of the existence which Eve and Adam would have once known, reared on the sweetness and light of perfected nature for the short duration of their lives, only able to keep paradise but for a short time. Milton's epic is not nature writing—it's post-nature writing. A poem which conveys the understanding that Eden may not be real—perhaps it never was, though its certainly not an actual location on the map right now—but that this beautiful, abstract idealization remains holy in the human soul, a blessed "No Place," a utopia. That dream of being totally in tune with nature, of perfect synchronization, if always a myth at least a potent one. When Milton had finished *Paradise Lost,* London was already a metropolis of well over a million people, the confines of the capital packed with human beings, streets filled with horse and human shit, lye clogging the Thames, soot, smog, and industrial run-off punctuating everyone's lives, where as Emily Cockayne writes in *Hubbub: Filth, Noise and Stench in England,* the "infrastructural development could not keep pace and parts of the city became increasingly crowded, dirty, and noisy." For those trapped within the urban jail of London, the New World did seem a paradise—the promise of a fresh, green continent without pollution, without enclosure, without the fallen-ness. Seven years after Milton died, and his fellow nonconformists the Quakers were granted a land charter by the king to establish their utopia of Pennsylvania, the largest proprietary holding on earth. By 1775, the first anthracite coal would be discovered in the province, and miners "Ransack'd the Center, and with impious hands / Rifl'd the bowels of thir mother Earth," as Milton wrote in his first book, men having "Op'nd into the Hill a spacious wound." The first steel would be produced a century after that, with Carnegie's Edgar Thompson facility still visible from the Monongahela just a hike through the park and the woods, for "There stood a Hill not far whose griesly top / Belch'd fire and rowling smoak; the rest entire / Shon with glossie scurff, undoubted sign / That in his womb was hid metallic Ore, / The work of Sulphur."

Book VIII—Influence

To ask or search I blame thee not for Heav'n
Is as the Book of God before thee set,
Wherein to read his wondrous Works, and learne
His Seasons, Hours, or Days, or Months, or Yeares.
                    —*Paradise Lost*, Book VIII

Literature is not exhaustible, for the sufficient and
simple reason that a single book is not. A book is
not an isolated entity: it is a narration, an axis of
innumerable narrations.

                    —Jorge Luis Borges, *Other Inquisitions*

Mary Godwin's monster first announced himself to her in a dream, while she stayed in the drafty environs of Villa Diodati along the shores of Lake Geneva, sometime in the middle of the night in the midst of a violent storm during that frigid summer of 1816 when the massive eruption of the volcano Mount Tambora half-a-world-away in Indonesia ensured that winter would last at least a whole twelve months. Only eighteen at the time, Godwin was traveling with her future husband—the Romantic poet Percy Shelley—as well as the writer and physician John Polidori, and their confidant and friend the brilliant, mad, bad, and dangerous to know Lord Byron, who had a whiff of Miltonic Sulfur about him. Ensconced by the fire within Villa Diodati, built a century earlier and named for and owned by the family of Charles Diodati, Milton's Swiss Italian school-age friend and arguably the only real love of his life, the four stayed up late discussing philosophy. Haunted by the presence of Milton within the estate's cream-colored walls, the four

English writers were spurned to a ghost story contest by Byron. Reading gothic stories and supernatural folk tales, Byron argued that a bit of the fantastic was what was called for on this blustery evening.

As the other participants stared into that hypnotic fire, perhaps warming themselves with cherry kirsch, Godwin felt herself blocked, inspiration somewhere at the edge of her mental peripheral vision, but unable to yet formulate her story into words. A few nights later, in the early morning, shutters banging against opaque windows, wind howling down from the Alps, Godwin suddenly had a terrifying vision: "I saw the pale student of unhallowed arts kneeling beside ... [a] hideous phantasm of a man stretched out, and then, on the working of some powerful engine, show signs of life, and stir with an uneasy, half vital motion." During the earlier fireside nocturne, Godwin had brought up the popular subject of Galvanism, the belief that application of electrical current would be able to reanimate dead flesh. Upon waking from her nightmare, Godwin quickly sketched out that embryonic tale that had been gestating in her skull, the narrative about a Swiss scientist who stitched together decomposing parts of various cadavers, this hobbled human chimera than endowed with life by lightning, a transgression to "mock the stupendous mechanism of the Creator," as she wrote. Two years later and the entire thing would be published as *Frankenstein; or, the Modern Prometheus*, printed under her married name of Mary Shelley. The epigraph would be from *Paradise Lost*—"Did I request thee, Maker, from my clay/To mould me man? Did I solicit thee/From darkness to promote me?"

Frankenstein is a thoroughly Miltonic novel. Like many of the Romantics, Shelley was inspired by the model of Luciferian rebellion which *Paradise Lost* supposedly advocated for, and her "Modern Prometheus" of the titular Viktor Frankenstein is a character who embodies certain Satanic virtues and vices, a figure of both inspiration and hubris. More than that, however, *Frankenstein* is also what she described it as in her reminiscence about its composition, a tale about mocking the creative powers of the Lord. Little about the scientist's work bares much similarity to the stolid and sober labor of empirical observation and experimentation, but Frankenstein's task does recall that of the model of the inspired artist, a Romantic obsession that owed much to both Milton and his character of Lucifer. Peter Conrad argues in his study *Creation: Artists, Gods & Origins* that *Frankenstein's* central myth is of the "genius whose rebellion drives the world we still live in ... an artist who unleashes the incubi inside his head," but this narrative owes everything to Milton's Satan, and arguably his God as well. Shelley's fascination with Milton is well-known, as is the indebtedness of the entire English Romantic movement to their forebearer. We know that she read *Paradise Lost* at least four times in her life, twice before she began working on *Frankenstein.* Her husband Percy had a similar attraction to

Milton, his radical poem *Prometheus Unbound* both evoking Satan and conflating him with the not dissimilar figure from Greek mythology. Just as obvious as Shelley's epigraph in *Frankenstein* is the scene in which the monster teaches himself how to speak and read English after he discovers a satchel of books, the most prominent one our familiar epic. "*Paradise Lost* excited different and far deeper emotions," the monster says, explaining that he read it as a true history. "Like Adam, I was apparently united by no link to any other being in existence; but his state was far different from mine in every other respect." Hence Shelley's contention that hers is about the risks of non-divine creation, for Adam is molded from the red earth of Mesopotamia and is imbued with sacred breath, but any such golem made by man must always be mere copy of a copy, and that includes our writing. Every work of literature must ultimately be a failed work of literature. That, it must be said, is not a reason to stop attempting literature, but an acknowledgment of creation's ever deferred perfection. God and Milton, Shelley and Frankenstein, all share a methodology since nothing is ever truly ex nihilo in creation. Shelley explained that *Frankenstein* is about how "parts of a creature might be manufactured, brought together, and imbued with vital warmth," but that's also an exact description of every writer's process, of how every work of literature is ultimately a stitched together monster from the corpses of other creatures.

Every work of art is fundamentally about creation, just

as every work of literature is about writing—and reading. The two are inextricably as combined as the branches of a double-helix, for all true writing is a process of grappling with that which you've read before, and for every author the act of reading is fuel for the future process of writing. Conrad notes that the "artist's brain, as Mary Shelley saw it, resembles that gulf of unebbing where the elements were mixed before cosmic order pacified them: 'dark, shapeless substances' murkily boiled and bubbled" where the author's creations should be understood as "brain-children." How Miltonic is this model, order arising from Chaos, the blessedness of creation only possible by building upon the raw material of that which precedes you? God—Frankenstein—Shelly—Milton. All of their creations were composites of things which existed before, true of every artist and every writer. *Frankenstein* was sutured together out of numerous influences, poems and novels which Shelley had read before. *Paradise Lost* stitched to Blake like a dismembered leg attached to a different torso; the treatises of Goethe sewn to the poetry of Galvani like a purpled head stapled to a corpuscular body. Every novel, every poem, is exactly the same way. Literature abhors a vacuum; in fact, it can't even recognize one. All writing is nourished by the rich soil of that which came before, same as it ever was. The dogma of ex nihilo creation has its aesthetic corollary with the myth of the singular genius, the creator who is not of his time but for all times, and yet nobody can be removed from the circumstances in which they were born, and whether or not the fingerprints of influence are obvious in one's writing, they are definitely there. We are all demiurges, creating in a universe not of our own construction, and there is no single God above us, it's just demiurges all the way down.

With a relative surfeit of biographical detail on Milton, literary historians can be relatively certain of the sources which he used, the readings that he thrilled too, the poets whom he imitated and was inspired by. By the seventeenth-century, knowledge was becoming fragmented and disparate enough that it was rapidly reaching a point at which it would be impossible for a single individual to be equally conversant in every possible discipline. Milton is perhaps the last person who was capable with equal facility to be brilliant in prosody and physics, legal theory and ancient history, comparative mythology and a dozen foreign language, so that *Paradise Lost* is the final of a type, an artifact from the last of the Renaissance men, a relic from a time when somebody could be the smartest person on earth. And all of that knowledge was filtered into his epic, so that Milton's poem is in a very straightforward way a book that's about other books, a text which is a record of reading. Recipient of a solid Renaissance humanistic education, Milton was encouraged to keep what's called a "common place book," that is a manuscript in which a reader might collect quotes that intrigue them, a place where they could copy out poems, and dialogue, and prose which was significant (and where often people would alter or "improve" the original). Known in the Middle Ages as *florilegia*, as the "flowers of reading," commonplace books were bouquets of ideas; intellectual gardens where thinkers could copy and rearrange, experiment and explore, edit, and revise. At some 250 pages of ink-stained bound paper with lines scratched out and certain phrases underlined, Milton's commonplace book is stored at Trinity College, Cambridge. Maintaining the practice throughout the tumultuous decades of the 1630s and 1640s as England imploded into civil war, and Milton's commonplace book records his deep engagement with theology, philosophy, and political theory, in addition to literature, all of that learning being evident within his most famous poem.

In examining a concordance of Milton's commonplace book prepared by the editor Ruth Mohl in 1969, seven dozen different writers stand out. The great Italians are there, Ariosto with his epic *Orlando Furioso*, Giovanni Boccaccio's eerie biography of Dante, the masterful Florentine himself (of course), that cynic of realpolitik Nicolo Machiavelli, the proto-Protestant zealot Girolamo Savonarola, Tasso's *Il Goffredo*, and so on. Rather predictably Milton is conversant with a stunning array of theological writings, ancient and contemporary, Catholic and Protestant. Augustine's sin-drenched ruminations, Clement of Alexandria, John Chrysostom, Tertullian's joyous irrationalism, Eusebius's church histories, even the founder of the hated Jesuits

Ignatius de Loyola. And his fellow countrymen are well-represented, with extensive notes on Geoffrey Chaucer's *The Canterbury Tales,* the Medieval poet John Gower, the great chronicler of the nascent empire Raphael Holinshed, Samuel Purchas's accounts of colonial exploration, Raleigh's *History of the World,* the Platonic and Protestant poetry of Philip Sidney, and his model myth-builder Spenser. His notes are prepared in English and Italian, Latin and Greek, the closest that we'd ever have to encountering Milton's exact unfiltered brain. Mohl writes, in a manner sadly avoided by contemporary academics, that "A good man by some reckoning seems to surpass even the angels, to the extent that, enclosed in a weak and earthly body always struggling with his passions, he nevertheless aspires to lead a life like that of the inhabitants of Heaven." Maybe. When it comes to his reading, certainly, Milton aspired to something transcendent, and if the weak and earthly body was a paper one, that collection of pages on which he recorded his thoughts, then it gestures toward a realm beyond, and the poem is its angelic progeny. Thus like every work of literature, *Paradise Lost* is a record of previous reading. It's just that the man who wrote it happened to have opened a lot of books. But just as Milton took free-floating globs of Tasso and Ariosto, Dante and Chaucer, Spenser and Shakespeare— the Bible—and concocted something novel out of it as if creation arising out of the firmament, so too has *Paradise Lost* become a constituent element in the literature and consciousness of those inspired by the poet. Though it's been quipped that *Paradise Lost* is more respected than read, a poet doesn't reach the stature of Milton without their syntax being passed down into English sentences, their diction into paragraphs, their ideas into our heads. Authors as disparate as Charlotte Brontë, Herman Melville, and Salman Rushdie all bear the imprimatur of their Miltonic creator.

Charlotte, Emily, and Anne's father, Rev. Patrick Brontë, made *Paradise Lost* a mainstay of family reading. Milton's influence runs through the women's work, but never more obviously than in *Shirley,* Charlotte's novel after *Jane Eyre.* Written a year after the tumultuous revolutions of 1848, *Shirley* took place in that similarly revolutionary year of 1812 when Luddites smashed capitalism's demonic machinery, which had begun to crowd and pollute the Yorkshire countryside where the novel takes place. With the backdrop of both Romantic revolution and the postlapsarian machinations of industry, *Shirley* calls to mind Hell's capital of Pandemonium, where the demon Mulciber tends the "fiery Deluge, fed / With ever-burning Sulphur unconsum'd." The master of Brontë's Pandemonium is Robert Moore, a northern English textile factory owner, whose livelihood has been threatened by the ban on exportation of cloth to America due to the War of 1812. Moore courts the wealthy and headstrong Shirley as a potential solution to his economic woe and in their conversations Brontë provides a defense of Eve, while recognizing the emancipatory kernel at the core of *Paradise Lost*. Brontë was a keen reader of Dr. Johnson's literary criticism, in particular his contention that Milton "thought woman made only for obedience, and man only for rebellion." With Milton's chauvinism in mind, Shirley inquires, "Milton was great; but was he good?" Shirley revises Milton's myopic portrayal of Eve, preferring to see her as a "woman-Titan," claiming, "Milton tried to see the first woman; but ... he saw her not." But despite that myopia, Brontë discerns a subversive thread underneath the surface of *Paradise Lost*.

For Melville, If *Paradise Lost* was a poetic consideration of the darker things in the psyche, of a megalomaniacal single-mindedness that pushed its antagonist into the very bowels of Hell, then Melville's obsessed Captain Ahab is our American Lucifer. As Lucifer stalks *Paradise Lost*, so Melville's novel is haunted by Ahab, that "grand, ungodly, god-like man." Melville claimed, "We want no American Miltons," but it was an unconvincing declaration, considering that he basically became one himself. Just as Lucifer would struggle with God and be cast into Hell, and Ahab would wrestle with Moby-Dick and be thrown into the Pacific, so would Melville grapple with Milton, though the results were perhaps not quite damnation. Yet he did write in a letter to his friend Nathaniel Hawthorne, that "I have written a wicked book, and feel as spotless as the lamb," and that his novel had been "broiled" in "hell-fire." Melville, it would seem, was of the Devil's party, and he very much knew it. *Moby-Dick*, of course, drew from seemingly as many sources as *Paradise Lost*, from literature, myth, and scripture, not to speak of the tawdry sea accounts that provided the raw materials of his narrative. *Moby-Dick*'s narrator, Ishmael, claims that he has "swam through libraries," and so too did Melville, but it was *Paradise Lost* that floated upon those waves as his white whale. The whale, of course, has always been configured as more than just a mere symbol, variously and ambiguously having his strange, great, empty white hide as a cipher potentially standing in for God, or the Devil, or America, or the very ground of Being. But where Lucifer is so comprehensible in his desires as to almost strike the reader as human, Melville's whale is inscrutable, enigmatic, sublime—far more terrifying than the shockingly pedestrian God as depicted by Milton. These two texts in conversation with one another across the centuries provide an almost symphonic point and counter point; for what Melville gives us is an atheistic *Paradise Lost* and is all the more terrifying for it.

Salman Rushdie's *The Satanic Verses* begins *in media res* just as Milton's poem does with a Luciferian fall. Somewhere above the English Channel an Indian jetliner explodes from a terrorist's bomb and from the flaming wreckage Gibreel Farishta and Saladin Chamcha "plummeted like bundles." The Bollywood actors are both miraculously condemned to an "endless but also ending angelicdevilish fall," which signaled the "process of their transmutation." What follows in Rushdie's fabulist novel of magical realism are a series of dream visions, where along the way Farishta, true to his given name, begins to resemble the archangel Gabriel and Chamcha finds himself transformed into a devil. The fall of these angels conjures the losing war against God before creation, when "headlong themselves they threw / Down from the verge of Heav'n," and as Chamcha becomes a devil, the formerly beautiful Lucifer transformed into Satan. Milton's theology could be strident, as indeed so is that of the post-colonial, secular Islamic atheist Rushdie. The latter famously found himself on the receiving end of a *fatwa* issued by the Ayatollah Ruholla Khomeini concerning perceived blasphemy regarding depictions of the prophet Muhammad, precipitating a decade of self-imposed hiding. An anxiety that Milton knew well, as he could have easily ended up on the executioner's scaffold. Any author with their own visionary theology risks being a heretic to somebody, illustrating the charged danger of religion. Scripture, after all, is simply the literature that people are willing to kill each other over. Milton's threat of persecution was largely political, while Rushdie's was explicitly religious, but that's just to quibble. Religion and politics are two categories which are inseparable, both in Milton's era and our own. Both men illustrate how writers can be the weather vanes of society, sensitive toward the changing fortunes of potential tyranny, and often victim to it as well. Rushdie once said in an interview, "Two things form the bedrock of any open society—freedom of expression and rule of law," a hard-won bit of wisdom and a sentiment that is a worthy descendant of Milton's argument for free-speech in his 1644 pamphlet *Areopagitica,* where he wrote that "he who destroys a good book, kills reason itself."

What of my own writing, Milton's presence in my words and sentences, my thinking? If we're all assemblages of that which we've read, then the poet holds a bigger than normal share of my attention ever since I flipped through the Norton in McIlvaine. He's in the exceedingly rarefied company of a handful of writers whose books I'd wish for if stranded on a desert isle, joined perhaps by the complete works of Shakespeare, Walt Whitman's *Leaves of Grass,* maybe the Bible (but probably not the last one). More than any of them I'd be happy with an eternally charged iPod, if I'm being honest (a denigration of literature in favor of music that was positively scandalous when I voiced it at the bar while in my PhD program, and yet I think the lyrics of Bob Dylan, Leonard Cohen, Joni Mitchell, Shane McGowan, and the Boss could sustain me for a while in that regard). Certainly, I see a poor aping of Milton's prose in my own writing, along with those other maximalist partisans of the lugubrious seventeenth-century sentence in the form of Robert Burton's *The Anatomy of Melancholy* and Thomas Browne's immaculate *Religio Medici.* Virtually nothing that Milton wrote in his prolific assortment of pamphlets would pass muster with those puritans of plain style Strunk and White;

he is enthused with semicolons and abundant clauses separated by copious commas, and his byzantine syntax can be as confusing as a labyrinth. So grandiose is Milton's diction that he often took to inventing his own Latinate neologisms, and he wore his learning in a manner that was pedantic, bordering on pretentious. None of those are vices in my mind, because to write in this way is to self-declare which ideas are your own, to stake ownership over something unique, to demand your own voice. To write in plain style is to conform, to sound like everyone else. There's one way to write as a minimalist, but to write as a maximalist is to let a thousand purple flowers bloom. When it comes to Milton's beliefs—whatever they might be—and how they've influenced me? That's an entirely more confusing quandary.

Book IX—Politics

Who can impair thee, mighty King, or bound
Thy Empire?

—*Paradise Lost*, Book VII

Milton! thou shouldst be living at this hour:
England hath need of thee.

—William Wordsworth, "London, 1802"

Before he ascended the scaffold, laid his head down and had it severed from his neck, King Charles I requested an extra shirt, so that he wouldn't shiver from the cold and convey the misapprehension that he was afraid to die. To be an executed king was shameful enough. To be a mocked, spurned, and laughed at king was entirely worse. Transferred from St. James Palace to the Banqueting House where he'd once dispensed his monarchical authority in the lushness of divine mandate, and in the winter of 1649 Parliamentarian forces had sentenced him to death, their verdict that he had upheld in "himself an unlimited and tyrannical power to rule according to his will, and to overthrow the rights and liberties of the people." Charles was not an indiscriminate libertine like his son, but he did suffer from two deadly, irreconcilable vices: the first being that he actually believed in the divine mandate and the second that he wasn't particularly bright. In his undershirt and black cloak framed with a blue sash— filthy, exhausted, and prepared to die—Charles gave a speech about how in Heaven an "uncorruptible crown" awaited him. An anonymous hagiographical pamphlet entitled *Eikon Basilike* reports that the king prayed that God should "look upon my misery with Thine eye of mercy and let Thine infinite power vouchsafe to limit out some proportion of deliverance unto me." Thomas Herbert, Guardian of the Bedchamber, said that it was "the saddest sight England ever saw." Milton saw something else—a foolish plagiarist. As Milton observed in *Eikonoklastes*, a rejoinder to royalist attempts at canonization, Charles prayer was originally from Sidney's romance *The Countess of Pembrooke's New Arcadia*. Even in his last moments, the dim monarch was unable to say a single genuine thing, rather stealing some words from a "vain amatorius poem."

Milton's politics still have the power to shock. He's always had an uncomfortable position in Britain, that preternaturally conservative nation, because he advocated for the decapitation of their king (who suffered due severance, though hardly because of Milton alone). Whether you think of that series of internecine wars between Cavalier Royalists and Parliamentary Roundheads as the "English Civil War" or the "English Revolution" depends on your politics. Conservative historians tend to minimize the radicalism of that decade, while those of a Marxist caste have long described it as a "revolution," prefiguring the American, French, and Russian turns. Christopher Hill describes it as a time of "great overturning, questioning, revaluing of everything in England" in his classic *The World Turned Upside Down: Radical Ideas During the English Revolution.* Regicide on the block rather than the battlefield had been unthinkable up until the moment the blade hit Charles' neck. Even Parliamentarians originally considered themselves loyal subjects, arguing that the civil war was an attempt to save Charles from the machinations of counselors like the hated Archbishop of Canterbury William Laud. Charles I prefigures Louis XVI beneath the guillotine or Nicholas II facing Bolshevik bullets, yet the English experiment in radical republicanism has been obscured, and Milton has been a casualty of that minimization. There are several reasons for this; for one, the English Revolution was unsuccessful, the Commonwealth government in shambles and Charles II on the throne in just a little over a decade. Even the Soviet Union went for seventy years. Because the Commonwealth wasn't enduring, it's occupied an odd place in British memory, a literal Interregnum. Today, there is a statue of Cromwell in front of the Parliament which the Queen opens every year. Secondly, much as Napoleon dissipated the initial hope of the French Revolution and Stalin that of the Russian, Cromwell acted as a tyrant far in excess of the executed king, an austere pseudo-monarch, hardened in battle and glorying in authoritarianism and death.

Finally, the language of religion and faith camouflages revolutionary potential, with Frank McLynn arguing in *The*

Road Not Taken: How Britain Narrowly Missed a Revolution, 1381–1922 that "vulgar Marxism has sometimes been too ready to conclude that religion must always be the opium of the people, or the fantasy of Man afflicted by his own inadequacy," dismissing the radical faith of that broad coalition of Parliamentarians as an "epiphenomenon." This is by far the most egregious of errors, for though it's true that politics and religion were inextricably combined, nothing about the latter was mere mask for the former, nor should we be so absurd as to assume that our own politics today aren't equally enmeshed in faith, whether it be Christian Nationalism, free market libertarianism, neoliberalism, or social democracy. Nothing is singular about the English Revolution's religiosity; French anticlericalism has confused how profoundly religious *that* revolution was, with its various schismatic faiths, whether the Cult of Reason or the Cult of the Supreme Being. A deep sense of prophetic transcendence motivated everything from the storming of the Bastille to the Reign of Terror. It's only a historical fallacy that configures the French Revolution as both more radical than the English and as the origin of secularism, though the first point is incorrect and the second assumes that something called "secularism" is even possible. More than that, the English Revolution had a radical promise that was snuffed out by Cromwell, a counter history of far more subversive currents having been entertained for a time.

Nonconformist groups with evocative names like the

True Levellers and the Ranters advocated for the complete equality of all humans, the redistribution of wealth, and the abolition of private property. Hill describes the contours of "another revolution which never happened," where radicals had "established communal property, a far wider democracy . . . [and which] might have disestablished the state church and the protestant ethic," where there would have been a rejection of "private property for communism . . . based on the fullest respect for the individual." Where then of Milton in that mad scrum, this period of prophets and poets, ravers and ranters, when armies upon the English mores dreamed of a millennial kingdom on earth, where God himself would liberate the proletariat? Educated and firmly bourgeois, Milton wasn't among the most zealous, men like Gerard Winstanley and his True Levellers who demolished the hedgerows that enclosed private farms so that the earth itself could be a common treasury of the destitute. Nor was his rhetoric that of Abiezzer Coppe, the prophetic pamphleteer whose grammar is stretched to the breaking point, his diction hermetic, his punctuation occult, his syntax schizophrenic. And Milton's role in the Commonwealth government, as it quickly evidenced an enthusiasm for the hierarchies that it had overthrown, the revolution eating itself (as those things tend to do), is an ethically complicated one. Yet despite all of those caveats, Milton is a man whose heart beat a bit faster for the mad ones, the extreme ones, the zealous, fanatical, crazed ones, those who refuse to accept tradition, authority, or the status quo. "Give me the liberty to know, to utter, and to argue freely according to conscience, above all liberties," he writes in *Areopagitica*.

By the time *Paradise Lost* was written, Milton's own revolution had already failed, overturned with surprising rapidity as Cromwell's son failed miserably in his role as Lord Protector, and then as Parliament invited Charles II back from Versailles where he'd been in exile. On Oak Apple Day in 1660 the new king returned to London, resplendent in silk and fur, feather and velvet, a decadent Francophile who situated himself as the opposite of everything which the Puritans had stood for. That Milton narrowly avoided execution speaks to the generosity of his friends like Marvell who advocated for him with the new regime, as well as the insulation of his own poetic fame. His survival was no certainty; for months the poet was in hiding, expecting to he arrested, tried, convicted, and killed. Though not a regicide himself, Milton's own words about the previous king's death—harsh, cutting, fanatical, mocking—wouldn't endear him to that same king's son. But he survived, was pardoned and forgiven, even if despondent in the failures of the "Good Old Cause" of the Commonwealth government. While Marvell and Dryden genuflected before the new order, Milton refused to abandon his republican convictions, writing during the year of the Restoration in *The Ready and Easy Way to Establish a Free Commonwealth* that "monarchy of itself may be convenient to some nations, yet to us who have thrown it out, received back again, it cannot be prove pernicious."

Blind, despondent, and harassed, as the revolutionary government was in free fall Milton admitted that he had "spoken only to trees and stones; and had none to cry to, but with the Prophet, *O earth, earth, earth!* to tell the very soil itself, what her perverse inhabitants are deaf to." *Paradise Lost* is about a failed rebellion and was written in the long dusk of Milton's own failed rebellion. Is Satan supposed to be Cromwell? For the throngs who lined the streets to catch a glimpse of Charles' retinue that answer is easy. By the eclipse of Interregnum, Milton's own enthusiasms for Cromwell had dimmed, he saw in that office which the dictator established that their revolution had been subverted. But *Paradise Lost* is no simple allegory, it's not George Orwell's *Animal Farm*. If the Serpent is Cromwellian that doesn't mean he's Cromwell. Nor should it be forgotten that Milton remained an unrepentant republican, that whatever his private misgivings, he would not bend the knee to a new king either. His poem is missive from the failed revolutionary who does not give up on revolution. If there is any of the confession in *Paradise Lost*, an awareness of how he was seduced by Cromwellian evil, then it's unclear whether it's conscious or not. It's possible that he had been of the Devil's party for a time, and he knew it. Perhaps *Paradise Lost* was an apology of sorts, not for the revolution but for the false messiah of that revolution, an explanation of how we can hew to a tyrant when he says what we want to hear, when his brutality is dressed in beautiful words. On our shelf of those revolutionaries who were so consistent in their hatred of tyranny that they could recognize it in their own breast, we'd have to place *Paradise Lost* next to Orwell's *Nineteenth Eighty-four,* next to Arthur Koestler's *Darkness at Noon.* What separates these men from the tin-pot authoritarians who always connect themselves to the fight for liberty is that they are conscious of the fact that revolutions must not just be fought on the field, but also in the soul.

Enmeshed in Renaissance political theory from Machiavelli to the Scotsmen George Buchanan, who advocated for the peoples' right to revolution, Milton's ideology is stunningly modern, even while his language is steadfastly biblical and his thoughts are abundantly religious. During the civil wars and through the Interregnum, Milton was known far more for his prose than his poetry, prolifically cranking out dozens of pamphlets on a multitude of controversial issues, and developing a reputation as a foaming revolutionary. His 1641 *Of Reformation* argued against episcopacy in a nation where Charles' father King James I had warned "No bishop, no king." This was followed with four more pamphlets vehemently denouncing church governance. Drawing from his own chaotic personal life, Milton penned *Doctrine and Discipline of Divorce* in 1644, a sustained proposal for the reform of marriage laws. That was the same year *Areopagitica* came out, the title a reference to the Athenian hill where oratory was unregulated, with

Milton's work the first sustained declaration in favor of free speech. With the blood still red on the sawdust at Whitehall, Milton published *The Tenure of Kings and Magistrates* two weeks after Charles's execution, fuming that nobody "can be so stupid to deny that all men naturally were born free, being the image and resemblance of God himself." Central to such a politics is the sense of divinity, that there is something sacred in rights.

If all of the talk about cutting the king's head off has made Milton an ambiguous figure in his native country, then that God-talk has made the left uncomfortable about claiming him as one of our own. Che, Lenin, Robespierre, even Jefferson—those seem like revolutionaries, but Milton's steadfast theological and scriptural language can't help but make many leftists take the safety off their Brownings. The Marxists who enthuse over much of the English Revolution start to blanch when all of those biblical references come out; as brilliant a historian as Hill would conclude that radicals of the seventeenth-century simply had *"illustrated* from the Bible conclusions at which they had arrived by rational means," that scripture was "used to illustrate truths of which one was already convinced." Yet when Winstanley, leader of the True Levellers, set up his commune at St. George's Hill, he wrote that the "earth should be made a common treasury of livelihood to all mankind, without respect of persons," and he wasn't drawing from secular philosophy, but rather from Acts 4:32. Men like Winstanley and Milton "believed" their Bibles, but what that verb meant isn't necessarily what folks might think it means today (chief of all those faithful to the twins of fundamentalism and atheism). His religion and politics weren't muddled, they were inseparable. Radicals like Milton believed in the power of turning the world upside down, of burning away the injustices and inequities of society, of divine rebellion. If their utopia has the odor of paradise that's because those two concepts are identical. The fact is that "religion" has often been reduced to mere issue of belief, of whether one ascents or not to a given dogma, creed, or doctrine, but faith is much more complicated than that. Religion partially does have to do with belief, but it also has to do with culture, language, identity. It has to do with the food you eat, and the clothes you wear; the company you keep, and how you decorate your home. More than anything, religion has to do with ultimate value, with the transcendent, with the numinous, and with how one orients themselves toward meaning. Politics and religion aren't just connected, they're inextricably bound. They're the same thing, or maybe more correct to say that the former is just an aspect of the latter, because ultimately *everything is a religion.* This, I've found, is a contention which too many of my fellow-traveling progressives, liberals, and leftists don't intuit. We've a fallacy of thinking that our opponents are rational, *that we're rational,* and it's long hobbled us.

On a drizzly day in November of 2016, with bloodshot eye and shaking hand, I walked through the cold sleet rain past the ruins of industry which dotted the working-class neighborhood of south Bethlehem, a concrete desert which gave way to the pastoral oasis of Lehigh University where I was then in my final PhD year. Many of the students seemed indifferent to what had been announced early in the morning that day, some appeared jubilant, and the wisest ones understood that a tragedy had just occurred, a distinctly American tragedy. They huddled under awnings and porticoes of the gray granite Gothic buildings, having hushed and worried phone calls to home; others seemed to just wander in the rain, waiting to hear any words of consolation from the lame duck president (which were not forthcoming), any threatening words from the president-elect (which were). Hiking up the hill toward the English department, I made my way to the office of an adviser who taught me Milton, but seemed to miss something basic about the poet. We exchanged pleasantries in his book-lined office, desk covered in journals and notebooks, me at the doorway and he seated next to a window overlooking the long expanse of the valley toward the Poconos. He dismissed my worries, said that like everyone else on the campus that I was being hysterical. Though he hadn't voted for the president-elect, my adviser was unconcerned with that vulgar figure. Didn't I know that he used to be a New York Democrat? And sure, his opinions on women were paleolithic, but to think that he was a racist? And besides, lots of good people had voted for him. He assured me, in his wisdom, that this would be no worse than Reagan (as if that was good). I was apoplectic, shocked that he couldn't see this rising malignancy. As I write this, after Charlottesville, coronavirus, and the Capitol, I think that my prediction holds up. Why was I right and my professor wrong? Because I understood what we faced—a dark, occult, malevolent faith. And I understand that the only means of resistance is its own form of faith.

"John Milton should be judged by the standards of the twenty-first century," David Hawkes writes in the provocative *John Milton: A Hero of Our Time,* while Nigel Smith sees the long-dead poet as someone with whom people can "think through . . . contemporary dilemmas" as he argues in the audaciously titled *Is Milton Better Than Shakespeare?* I agree with both, though not perhaps in the literal sense. Milton has nothing directly to tell us about any of the political issues that dominate social media; he is not the prophet of wokeness or anti-wokeness, the bard of cancel culture or of free speech, the poet of culture war. Any aspect of the "discourse," liberal or conservative, would befuddle him because Milton lived three-hundred-and-fifty years ago! Milton was neither liberal nor conservative, Democratic or Republic, blue or red—he's a radical. I'm with Smith that we can think through many contemporary issues with *Paradise Lost,* and Hawkes has a point about judging the poet by our standards, but let's not treat an oracle like a mirror. If *Paradise Lost* has any political advice to impart in our quickly collapsing society, buffeted by climate change and incipient fascism, it's this—politics is merely religion by other means. Inheritors of the Enlightenment myth of secularism, we pretend as if any politics, be they right or left, conservative or liberal, can be easily separated from faith, but religion is only the question of ultimate value, and whether or not it has anything to do with the gods is an individual issue. At the genesis of the Age of Reason, Milton was not yet cursed by that fable of disenchantment and so he understood that all ideologies are at their core theologies, since they ask and answer the question "What is it that we are to serve?" Today we pretend that our positions are political rather than religious, but partisanship is just sectarianism by another name. If there is another lesson from *Paradise Lost* it's that our only means of resistance is always of faith, because the only things deserving of our struggle against them are the gods, whether they're dark or not. God and the Devil are both sacred, after all.

Book X—Eternity

For ever shall endure; the like shall sing
All Prophecie . . .

—*Paradise Lost,* Book XII

Where are your ancestors now?
And the prophets, do they live forever?

—Zechariah 1:5

Six weeks after I watched my father die of blood cancer and six weeks before I had the final drink of my rock bottom (so far), I read a dog-eared, underlined, broken-spined Dover Thrift Edition of Walt Whitman's *Leaves of Grass* while on Amtrack's *The Pennsylvanian*. Suddenly, while traveling from Manhattan to Pittsburgh, I approached an intimation of sun-dappled eternity. During the late afternoon golden hour of a pristine July day, in a valley of the Allegheny Mountains, the tracks ranging into a flatness ringed by green peaks, the diffraction of light flickering shade across the window, each visible tree leaf, mountain laurel, and stone in the brook running alongside us aglow, as if light emanated from within. That summer there was a sense of hurtling toward a shining, terrifying, beautiful, awful infinity. It began with my brother and me holding vigil by my unconscious father's hospice bedside for the only night he spent there after being admitted from the ICU. To bear such a witness is fathoms painful, and yet very necessary; a night watch among the most important hours of my life. Before my father died, I spent those last few minutes with him simply describing the Pittsburgh landscape visible from his window as the sun rose, the low roll of the red-bricked row houses as they slinked through Bloomfield and Friendship, the spires of churches and cathedrals in Shadyside and East Liberty. The night before, my brother, mother, and me had seen a lone hawk flying over that same scene, and it seemed an omen pregnant with significance. In the morning, my mother came, and I slipped out for a cup of coffee; my father died only a few minutes after that, listening to a Dave Brubeck CD.

That August ended with me unconscious on a Bethlehem, Pennsylvania sidewalk, halo of broken bottles and cashed cigarettes by my head, having laid down to look up at the stars. Not far from my apartment in an old Victorian building with copper-ringed windows, I passed out right where my steep street intersected with an industrial iron bridge. The police arrested me, hauled me into an ambulance, and sent me off to the emergency room. I was in a plaid sports coat and Allen Edmund wingtips; the whole way to the hospital I quoted Whitman (I think). In between that prologue and epilogue, I drank and read and barely survived. Untreated grief is a canker. I have no regrets about how my family tended to my dad in his last days—even though cancer is painful, unforgiving, and meaningless—my father had as near to a "Good Death" in the Medieval sense of the *ars*

Moriendi as we could provide. Love and "Blue Ronda ala Turk" are enough, after all. What I do regret are all of the conversations I can never have with my dad, all of the essays of mine that he'll never get to read, that he didn't get to come to my wedding, that he'll never get to meet my son. That he never saw me sober. Everything I've written since he died, on some level, has been an attempt to talk to him, to explain some interesting idea, or to show to him some fascinating subject that I've learned about. On that train, having left New York a few hours before where I stayed with my future wife, and I dutifully scribbled marginalia on those cheap Dover newsprint pages, when I had an opportunity to reread, and to finally, albeit briefly, understand something of what Whitman meant in these stanzas:

They are alive and well somewhere,
The smallest sprout shows there is really no death,
And if ever there was it led forward life, and does not
wait at the end to arrest it,
And ceas'd the moment life appear'd.

All goes onward and outward, nothing collapses,
And to die is different from what any one supposed,
and luckier.

This is not to say that before this particular moment that I couldn't have given you veritable dissertations on the significance of those stanzas, on Whitman's relationship to nineteenth-century Spiritualism and beliefs in reincarnation, on Swedenborgianism and the Second Great Awakening. But in that second all of that stuff was just words, words, words. For a brief and shining moment *I actually understood what it means that there is no death* and that to die is different from what one supposed, and luckier too. That's to say that Whitman is a poet, but for a sacred minute of my life he was also a prophet, too.

The word "prophecy" has unfortunate connotations, associated with tawdry magic and cheap predictions, astrology and tarot. In the biblical sense, a prophet is more than a divinator or soothsayer, though being able to tell the future is partially their purview. Scripturally a prophet is somebody who declaims unpleasant truths to power, and their predictions are of what shall befall God's people if they choose injustice. Fundamentally, the prophet has a political function, and prophets like Isaiah, Jeremiah, Elijah, and Zechariah bear little similarity to astrologers. Which isn't to say that the prophetic vocation doesn't have anything to do with the concept of time—it does. If a prophet is capable of seeing what may come that's only because the mode of prophetic writing exists beyond the confines of past, present, and future. A prophet isn't immortal, but a prophet is eternal. They write beyond space and time. Prophetic literature gives the reader an experience of that paradise which exists in a direction beyond time, in a different space. Small enough to dwell within an atom and brief enough to occur in a second, which is to say everywhere and for all time. When Whitman writes in his poem "On Crossing Brooklyn Ferry" that you who "shall cross from shore to shore years hence are more to me, and more in my / meditations, / than you might suppose," he is writing prophetically, not because he's seeing into the future from the past, but because he's abolished time itself. If read in the right dappled sunlight, you can hear his voice speaking to you. All literature is influenced by the context in which it's written, but prophetic writing breaks free of all that, even if for only an instant. Prophets and poets alike write from the perspective of deathless eternity.

Within Anglophone literature there are four great prophetic poets—Whitman, Dickinson, Blake, and Milton. Being able to convey something of eternity is not all of that which makes them great, nor can literary greatness be reduced to the prophetic. Plenty of poets and writers revel in the granular, the specific, the contingent, even as they eschew eternal concerns. For that matter, plenty of writers who do enmesh themselves in eternity might produce prophecy, but the writing itself is bad. Plenty of dissenters and nonconformists in Milton's own day wrote borderline psychedelic work capable of propelling you out of a sense of yourself, but the result is more idiosyncratic than brilliant. Aesthetics can't always be reduced into mysticism. When I argue that a poet like Whitman—or Milton—is prophetic, this must be separated from the humdrum observation that they're canonical. *Of course* they're canonical, but that merely has to do with what writers have been approved by those profane forces of economics, politics, and tradition. Canonization is an issue of who has been lauded, who has happened to survive the exigencies of literary history; it is an issue of sociology, not theology. When I say that a poet is prophetic, my claim is that their liturgy compels us—in the right circumstance—into a time without time, a space beyond space. In claiming these four as prophetic poets, I don't discount all of the unread verse that does something similar, perhaps something greater. The moldering moleskins kept in water-logged basements, the scratched marginalia in the borders of lost books, graffiti upon tenement walls, lines scratched out in South Carolina plantation dirt and on the concrete of the Warsaw ghetto. Works every bit the equal of Milton could be lost to us, but the forgotten have even a quieter voice than the anonymous, all of those obscured by entropy and tragedy. I can make such a claim about Milton, Blake, Whitman, and Dickinson because they happen to be remembered, and even if that is only due to luck, all the more grateful must we be. Prophets are like saints—there are many more than just the ones whom you can name.

Prosody is a tool of prophecy. Each one of those poets broke the traditional forms of verse, and in making it new they announced the radicalism of their visions. Milton's blank verse, Blake's obscure and hermetic metaphors, Dickinson's irreverence fit to the beat of a hymn, Whitman's free verse. The avant-garde is the mode of the prophet, for anything said in a mundane, or prosaic, or quotidian way cannot be prophecy. As Christ said in Mark 6:4, "A prophet is not without honor, but in his own country, and among his own kin, and in his own house." None of the poetic conceits of these poets were universally appreciated during their lifetimes. Whitman's long, unspooling, free-verse sentences and endless litanies were seen as barbaric, yawp or not; Dickinson's idiosyncratic punctuation was "corrected" by early editors; Milton's blank verse was uncouth and unpoetic, and Blake, when he was read, was often dismissed as a madman (which he was, of course, in the most beautiful sense). Because to write prophetically a poet's prosody must be pushed beyond the event horizon. Another lesson must also be drawn—every true prophet is a heretic. All four of these poets were God-intoxicated, but when one dwells in such a sacred extremity, when the holy is all of that which you see, hear, touch, smell, and taste, then you depart from the man-made rules of mere religion into something else. They skirt the edges of blasphemy, profanation, heresy. The heretic is a holy person because only they and the saint take the Lord seriously, everybody else is just concerned with appearances. The prophet-poet and the heretic imbibe not dogma but wonder. Hubert Dreyfus and Sean Dorrance Kelly in *All Things Shining: Reading the Western Classics to Find Meaning in a Secular Age* extol an engagement with literature that lures "back the shining things," that "uncover the wonder we were once capable of experiencing and to reveal a world that sometimes calls forth such a mood," as indeed was the experience I had on *The Pennsylvanian*.

When Whitman begins *Leaves of Grass* with "I celebrate myself, and sing myself, / And what I assume you shall assume, / For every atom belonging to me as good belongs to you" he provides a prophetic axiom, a democratic declaration that conflates our identities, that uses the second person perspective to speak across decades and miles. His voice, in the very first stanza of his greatest poem, is one that you hear in your head, that you listen to as your own voice, which is both what makes it so powerful and so singularly prophetic. Whitman's writing is abstracted, his poetry seemingly composed from a place beyond history, and like any true prophet, he's aware of that which shall pass and those things which are enduring. When "Song of Myself" was published to lackluster response, Whitman could still be content in knowing that he'd produced prophecy, for the voice of that poem speaks not just within but beyond as well. It's that sense of *eternity* which makes the difference here, and because of that there is an immortality which is lacking in verse which is not prophetic. There are certain similarities between Whitman and Milton; both are inheritors of the dissenting religious tradition; the former was a Quaker by birth and the latter was a fellow traveler of that sect. Both men had radical political allegiances, and both had a desire to break the shackles of conservative prosody. They were, it must be said, also profoundly different. Large hearted, earth-bestriding Whitman who seemed to gallop across the Hudson, the Schuylkill, the Potomac; whose mind ranged over the Alleghenies and the Appalachians, the Great Plains and the Rockies, who sang a song for the enslaved and the slaver alike, who wrote in the voice of the frontiersman and the Indian, the pauper and the President, seems rather distant from fussy, grumpy Milton in his drawing room. Yet Milton spoke in a register of eternity every bit as transcendent as Whitman, where as the former wrote in *Il Pensoroso*, "Till old experience do attain/To something like prophetic strain."

The seventeenth-century was a prophetic era, when the English Revolution catalyzed a creative reaction that arguably hadn't existed in Christianity since the Gnostics of the first few centuries. Groups like Baptists, Quakers, and Unitarians emerged out of these ruptures and the relative freedom of the period's chaos, but far more exotic denominations also thrived, many of whom treasured prophetic enrapture. "Thus saith the Lord, I inform you, that I overturn, overturn, overturn," wrote Abiezzer Cope in *A Fiery Flying Roll*. A contemporary of Milton's and a member of the group known as the Ranters, Coppe preached an antinomian gospel that found freedom in the death of archaic religious dogmas, even those of a traditional belief in God. The Ranters were joined by the Diggers, the Seekers, the Brownists, the Familiasts, and the Muggletonians who believed that God Himself had literally died, so that a new freedom could be born. As an angel says to Cope of this new prophecy, "Go up to London, to London, that great city, and write, write, write." An explosion of idiosyncratic religious material was promulgated in pamphlets, sermons, and broadsheets, the radical prophetic possibilities of renegotiating humanity's relationship with the sacred all up for argument. "And all man's preachings," writes Coppe, "hearing, teachings, learnings, holinesses, righteousnesses religions, is as Theft, Murder, and Adultery." As such nonconformists saw it, a new holiness could be born. The author of *Paradise Lost* must be understood as part of such a time. The language of prophecy is threaded through the earliest of Milton's verse, and it reaches its culmination in *Paradise Lost*. When he claims that he was inspired by Urania, or that the true voice of the epic is the Holy Spirit, this isn't a rhetorical conceit—he meant it. For him, the vocation of verse and of vision were reciprocal, for as John Spencer Hill writes in *John Milton: Poet, Priest, and Prophet,* "Milton's prophetic inspiration is the natural concomitant of his poetic inspiration."

True for all of my poet-prophets. Perhaps Dickinson alone was less boisterous in a declaration of chosenness, but even the Bard of Amherst in her cloistered anchorite's attic bore the stigmata of the true prophet (and importantly she knew it). All four of my poet-prophets lived in estimably prophetic times. Blake wrote in the midst of the Transatlantic series of revivals known as the First Great Awakening, but was really among the last of the dissenters of the old guard who raved and ranted in the London streets of Milton's day. Similarly, Whitman and Dickinson were inheritors of the religious fervor that burnt across the United States in the first half of the nineteenth century in what's known as the Second Great Awakening. Religious liberty allowed for a multitude of sects to thrive, from Millerites and Adventists to Spiritualists and Mormons, and both of the American poets in their own divergent ways spoke in the vocabulary of individual and occult concerns—what Harold Bloom in *The American Religion* describes as the "abyss of ecstasy." An abyss that isn't nihilistic, it should be affirmed, but rather a wholly and holy sacred Otherness, a nothingness. This is the perch above time, the singularity outside of space, from which the prophet can observe, and it's when their words as truly imparted allow for the reader to briefly approach eternity. Whitman does it in "Song of Myself" and "Crossing Brooklyn Ferry," with that personal address to readers—to you—from long after the poet himself has died, momentarily abolishing the tyranny of the past and future. Dickinson does it in her poem 591 when she writes "I heard a Fly buzz—when I died," the elevation of the present into an everywhere, her cryptic tense allowing the poet to briefly flicker alive once again in the reader's consciousness. Milton of course accomplished it in *Paradise Lost*, the epic in which the poet himself is witness to the creation of the world, standing outside of time and able to touch both Alpha and Omega with his hands.

Blake gives an apt summation of this perspective in "Auguries of Innocence" when he imagines the "World in a Grain of Sand / And a Heaven in a Wild Flower . . . Infinity in the palm of your hand / And Eternity in an hour." Like many poetic turns of phrase that are drained of their sublimity, tamed, and transformed into inspirational pablum, the full impact of Blake's aphorism can be obscured. Yet to read it freshly, with the naked and awesome eyelids of the morning, is to understand something about how the prophet is one who cannot die because the prophet lives beyond mere time. If eternity is in an hour, then paradise is now; if infinity is in the palm of your hand, than heaven is here. Blake's great forerunner was the poet of *Paradise Lost*, whom the former valorized in his own epic entitled *Milton: A Poem in Two Books*, both an examination of a prophet and a work of prophecy itself. Within *Milton*, Blake imagines the poet as returning to earth to "correct" his own theological mistakes, to reject any traces of Calvinism that otherwise infect the visionary quality of *Paradise Lost*. For Blake, as cracked and heretical a Christian as he may have been, all of the "Writings of Homer & Ovid, of Plato & Cicero" can't compare "against the Sublime of the Bible" which reaches its apotheosis with Milton. Yet the dross and fetters of authoritarian religion still contaminate *Paradise Lost*, and so Blake liberates Milton from heaven, he filches him from eternity, so that the redemption of the epic can be sustained through a radical rereading. "And thou

O Milton art a state about to be created/Called Eternal Annihilation that none but the Living shall Dare to enter," Blake tells his great influence, "they shall enter triumphant over Death/And Hell & the Grave: States that are not." The beautiful paradoxes of nothingness and eternity, this "place where contraries are equally true . . . a pleasant lovely Shadow, where no dispute can come, because of those who sleep." The font of all prophecy, that eternal place.

During the second half of 2007 I lived in Glasgow, at the eastern edge of that industrial city, in an apartment that overlooked the Victorian cemetery named the Necropolis. Frequently taking the train from the Buchanan Street Station, I spent dozens of afternoons in Edinburgh, exploring the craggy stone streets of the Medieval Old Town, the claustrophobic, winding alleyways of the ancient city as it slinked toward the castle which stood sentry over the green valleys of the capital. On one of these sojourns, I visited the Scottish National Gallery in the Georgian New Town, not far from the large crevice which bisected Edinburgh into two levels of its own history. The museum had mounted a modest but impressive exhibition of Blake watercolors, engravings and lithographs—the only poet equally proficient in visual art—and I spent a few hours crouched down in the dim light of the gallery examining his eccentric compositions. Here were the various imaginings of celestial beings whom Blake first espied as a young man, angels that filled the trees and gardens near his Lambeth home; the strange and terrifying depiction of a flea's soul, a reptilian creature bestriding across a dark landscape; and an illustration from *Milton* of its titular subject, the nude poet surprisingly taut and muscular with long gray hair, confronting the swirling vortices of the infinite. Some of Blake's most evocative illustrations are inspired by the Bible, and I was particularly drawn to his series about the sufferings of that righteous servant Job. With grave severity, the viewer can contemplate the many tortures of that man; the withering of his crops, the afflicting boils which he must scrape off with ash and pottery shard, the death of his beloved children. Finally, Blake shows us God in the whirlwind. Both Job and the Lord share the exact same elderly, wizened, and bearded face, as if they're the same person. A crucial lesson from Blake the prophet, who learned of it in the halls of eternity.

Book XI—Mind

The mind is its own place, and in itself
Can make a heav'n of hell, a hell of heav'n.
                    —*Paradise Lost*, Book I

MIND, n. A mysterious form of matter secreted
by the brain.
            —Ambrose Bierce, *The Devil's Dictionary*

Sometime in 1728, the Irish philosopher, minister, educator, and occasional poet Bishop George Berkeley must have adjusted his crisp, starched clerical collar over his dark ecclesiastical robes, placed his favored black, velvet turban over his shorn, egg-shaped head, and perambulated from his plantation Whitehall through the busy and pleasant streets of Newport. Having only recently arrived in the Province of Rhode Island and Providence Plantation, Berkeley availed himself of the religious independence in the Baptist colony to interrogate any number of beliefs, to posit a variety of new conjectures. He made plans for a utopian settlement to be established in Bermuda (it never was) and investigated drinking tar-water in treating gout; he wrote witty philosophical dialogues and theorized about the future providential greatness of American civilization, where "Westward the course of empire takes its way." Most of all, he read and wrote in Whitehall, contemplating the nature of mind, consciousness, and reality (with all of his physical cares provided by the several enslaved people whom he owned). "Truth is the cry of all," he would write sixteen years later in *Siris*, "but the game of the few."

Facing the Atlantic on Aquidneck Island, Berkeley's Whitehall was named after the same royal palace where the executed king had resided, and its neoclassical designs—soon to be common in American architecture—were drawn from the English designer Inigo Jones and the Venetian Andrea Palladio. Making his way down the pleasant slopping green of the hill, his feet steady on the pebbles and shells, Berkeley was drawn to the cliffs overlooking the ocean, for as he wrote to an associate in Dublin, Rhode Island "exhibited some of the softest rural and grandest ocean scenery in the world." Crouching on the grass, Berkeley gave himself over to a few minutes simply to exist here at the edge of the world; a cool breeze from the ocean blowing across the dome of the philosopher's scalp, the cawing of the sea gulls over the bay, glint of the orange sun as it melts into the water, sting of sweat in the Irishman's eye, smell of salt and the forever sound of the tide on the rocky shoals. So much beauty, and yet Berkeley understood that if he was by himself, and if he plugged his ears and closed his eyes, the whole world would cease to exist (that is if God also should look away, of course). His metaphysics, you see, commanded it.

There's an anecdote in Boswell's biography of Dr. Johnson that recounts how when the curmudgeonly lexicographer learned of the Irishman's philosophical argument which held that absolutely all matter was mere mental illusion—sensory data a type of dream rather than a reality—that Johnson kicked a rock and declared "I refute Berkeley thus." I've obviously reduced Berkeley's argument in the interests of narrative snark, but many philosophers in the eighteenth-century took his philosophy of *immaterialism,* that all of reality was subjective and idealist, very seriously. Many still think there is something to the radical empiricism of Berkeley, his claim that reality is an issue of perception, and that at its core the only things that are "real" are those things fixed in the kingdom of the mind. To be is to be perceived, Berkeley would argue, and his metaphysics does conform to our experience of this world, the gnawing sense that when you turn out the lights everything disappears except for yourself. Berkeley writes in *The Principles of Human Knowledge* that "sensible things are those only which are immediately perceived by sense," and since all that you experience—the heat from a Newport sun on your face, the smell of blue violets growing along the cliffside, the sound of crashing waves below, the feel of rocks and shells beneath your hands, the low roll of dark clouds over the ocean, the taste of salt spray—is mediated through your mind, it's logical to assume that it exists only there. No sun, violets, waves, rocks, clouds, or salt except for those that are imagined. From Plato to Borges there has been a metaphysical attraction among some philosophers to such idealism, but Berkeley's was among the most extreme, the contention that absolutely all of life is but a dream. For Berkeley, the fundamental unit of reality wasn't the atom, but rather the thought. What allows for the continuation of existence is the world's observation. The only reason we don't blink out of being is because there is an arch-Observer watching over us all, which the pious priest understood to be God.

There is a parsimonious elegance to Berkeley's thought, the sense of the universe as a thinking, contemplating, organic being, with the added bonus of all material limitations being eliminated as mere remainder, both our pleasures and our pains as illusory as a passing thought. During the Enlightenment, philosophers carried on a complicated and contentious series of debates about the relationship between the mind and matter. Bertrand Russell in *A History of Western Philosophy* explains that Berkeley relies "upon the received view that everything must be either material or mental, and that nothing is both," so that everything was actually the latter, but most thinkers during the seventeenth and eighteenth century hewed toward dualism, the position that reality is composed of two different substances, something material and something mental, even while the relationship between them was difficult to parse. René Descartes, the figure most associated with this dualism, conjectured that the soul interacted with the body through the pineal gland, while his contemporary Thomas Hobbes held the opposite of Berkeley's position, that everything was material (the ruling orthodoxy of scientific positivism in our contemporary era). Of course when you get to the constituent particles of either mind or matter, everything still runs up against an inscrutable abstraction. An atom can prove to be just as ephemeral as a granular thought, for what any of it actually means is forever deferred.

Central to *Paradise Lost* is the question of "What is consciousness?" While one might assume that Milton may have prefigured Berkeley's mystical idealism (the philosopher was only eleven when the writer died), most scholars agree that the poet embraced a radical materialism. Even though Milton is rarely included among Descartes and Hobbes, Berkeley and John Locke, his poem has as much to say about the relationship between mind and matter as *A Treatise Concerning the Principles of Human Knowledge*. Milton's *Paradise Lost* is an epic of embodiment, it's concerned with material things, with the sights, sounds, scents, and textures of the garden, with how the fall implies bodily frailty. Even his novel myth of creation, with God forming the firmament out of the inchoate *stuff* of Chaos, is materialist in a manner that ex nihilo genesis isn't. Milton had to grasp and feel along the walls of his cottage, unable to see or sense that which was always cloaked in perennial darkness, so that matter was always pertinent. The infirm don't have the privilege of metaphysical idealism. Stephen M. Fallon writes in *Milton Among the Philosophers* that the poet's "materialist monism treats spirit and matter as manifestations . . . of the one corporal substance. Milton's spirit does not coexist with alien matter; it contains matter." Put more succinctly, Milton's understanding of the world's composition is the opposite of Berkeley's. Both concur that there is only one substance, but Berkeley thinks that's all no matter while Milton pays it no mind. An incongruity in the ultimate Christian poet being an avowed materialist, even though the nature of his religiosity demonstrates repeatedly just how unusual the poet's piety was.

The conundrum of consciousness remains the most intimate metaphysical quandary, one where even if science has been able to further explicate how the brain works, philosophers are no more certain on how the mind operates than they were millennia ago. Neuroscientists have long embraced a physical materialism, assuming that our thoughts, feelings, and emotions arise from neurotransmitter reactions. Gone is spirit, noumena, and soul, replaced with serotonin and dopamine. And it should be said that there have been tremendous medical benefits to that assumption. Psychotropic drugs treat mental illness, brain surgeons can excise cancer and fix neurological disorders, and we understand how overall physical health contributes to psychological well-being. But for all of that, we're not really much closer to understanding *consciousness*. We might be able to use an MRI to chart an individual's brain waves when they listen to Bach's *Brandenburg Concerto* or to see what in Broca's region or the temporal lobe lights up as somebody reads *Paradise Lost,* but the subtle sifting of moods, the interplay of feeling, the interior, idiosyncratic, individual sense of what it feels like *to be*— all of that remains enigmatic. Ironically, the techno-utopians of Silicon Valley who are sometimes known as Transhumanists have embraced a monistic materialism so all-consuming that it comes around the other side and appears as Berkeley's idealism in scientific dross, with their belief that the human mind is reducible to the brain proffering the possibility of people being downloaded into computers, or artificial intelligence replicating consciousness. Resurrection of a soul under the guise of the physical. The question remains the same, however—is the universe composed of one thing, or two. If there are two such substances, how do we differentiate between "mind" and "matter," and how exactly do they relate to one another?

This chapter's epigraph is perhaps the most famous line from *Paradise Lost*, though like any cherry-picked sentence it's often yoked to sentiments that are perilously divergent from Milton's beliefs. Google a modernized version of the line (with the characteristic contractions of elision eliminated) and "The mind is its own place and can make a heaven of hell and a hell of heaven" will return results at less than scholarly sites including Tumblr and Pinterest, QuoteCatalogue and BrainyQuotes.com. An inquiry on Quora asking what Milton meant returns the following answer: "We each have the power . . . to make a choice . . . to have a 'great and positive' reality or a 'really horrible sucky victimized reality.'" At a website predictably titled *PositLive,* an author argues that "this quote also reminds us that it's within our power and mind to either find or create the good in bad situations." And at the *GoodNewsNetwork,* Milton's complicated digression about the relationship between mind and matter, illusions and reality, is the inspirational quote of the day for June 2, 2021. What all of these interpretations share is that they're saccharine, sentimental, and schmaltzy *bullshit.* Ripped from the narrative, suddenly Milton is made to read like Dale Carnegie, Norman Vincent Peale, Eckhart Tolle, Rhonda Byrne, or Oprah. American culture does what it always does, transforming gold into gild, taking wisdom—however ambiguously phrased—and making it into just one more bit of pablum about neoliberal bootstrapping, conservative rugged individualism, being self-made, and having a positive attitude. *Paradise Lost and the Seven Habits of Highly Effective People.*

What *Quora* fails to mention is that it's *Satan* who first utters that line, which complicates its Hallmark Card appropriateness. More importantly, it should make any reader question just how accurate its sentiment is, uttered by defeated Lucifer as he builds his infernal kingdom and begins to plan the temptation of humanity (which ends with him and his comrades transformed into hideous slithering serpents). But while we can dismiss any New Age positivity therein, it wouldn't be accurate to say that the line is only ironic either, for Milton's views about the relationship between mind and matter are productively ambiguous. Even while mainline Milton scholarship has long classified the poet as a steadfast materialist, he doesn't need to be as certain and definite as Hobbes or Berkeley on such issues. If we're to read Satan's axiom as a declaration of the complete sovereignty of the mind and its ability to overcome any physical limitations (even being in Hell), then obviously Lucifer is in error. By Book XII, the demonic hordes must understand that a positive attitude will only accomplish so much. For most of us, life itself demonstrates how much we're constrained by material circumstance; dreaming about being rich will not make me so, the heaven of my own mind can't transform me into Brad Pitt or Jon Hamm, no amount of dreaming will turn a Monongahela slag heap into Waikiki. And yet, it should be noted, the power of positive thinking certainly assisted Satan for a while. Nor, to take a slightly different tack, should it be obscured that the second half of the Milton line expresses a sobering truth—if the mind can elevate hell, it can just as easily denigrate heaven, as anyone with the summer blues understands.

Milton didn't disbelieve in the mind—it is it's own place, a *physical* descriptor, after all—but consciousness was situated within matter. Satan's great error is that he forgets that he is an embodied entity, that he is a creature of physical dimension, composed of matter like everything else. Not a small fallacy, nor an uncommon one today. So many of our dominant technological metaphors are idealist even while those same devices are based on materialist principles. We delude ourselves that the digital exists beyond matter, that our computers can make a heaven of hell, all the easier to ignore poisoned water, polluted air, and rising temperatures. Berkeley may have thought that the world disappeared when he closed his eyes, but the world never forgot about Berkeley. We may affirm the materialism that explains how silicon chips and transistors work, but our faith remains as gnostic as ever. That entire line of thinking which pretends that the world exists only in the mind, a venerable lineage running from Plato's "Allegory of the Cave" though *The Matrix*, can reach its most terrifying and logical conclusion with solipsism. Percy F. Bicknell describes this metaphysical position in *The Christian Register*, writing that the "solipsist claims to be the sole inhabitant of the universe, and all manifestations to the contrary are merely subjective states of his own . . . his cosmos is all ego." Insanity as metaphysics, and yet in attenuated forms we see solipsism in egoism, self-centeredness, narcissism. Satan's pride.

Lucifer understands himself to be the most important thing, and insomuch as he has any regard for the other demons, it's as extensions of himself, his solipsism veering into sociopathy. Yet if the mind is its own place, than being stuck there can be its own hell. Like many teenagers, I was terrified by the possibility of solipsism, what T.S. Eliot aptly described in *The Cocktail Party* when he wrote, "Hell is oneself./Hell is alone, the other figures in it/Merely projections. There is nothing to escape from/And nothing to escape to. One is always alone." I was disturbed by Philip K. Dick's fantasies of life being a computer simulation, or philosophical thought experiments with titles like "The Brain in a Vat Hypothesis." An irony is that if the mind as its own place happens to be the *only place* then, by definition, it's hell. Satan may have thrilled to the idea of being able to mold reality through his imagination, having desired such omnipotence, but that lonely perdition is a punishment which we reserve only for God. A clear answer to the solipsist's fear that they alone exist, that they're God, is the fairly commonsensical awareness that comes with maturity. You age out of solipsism. Maybe as a healthy and vigorous young man I could have worried that my mind was everything, but creaking joints, a bulging belly, poor eyesight, crap lungs, a shot liver, and an aching back have long ago convinced me that my mind can only do so much to make a heaven of hell without me getting on the Peloton.

Part of Milton's wisdom of embodiment, part of materialism's brilliance, is the understanding that you don't just think with your mind, but also with your stomach, your legs, your arms, your feet, your hands, your back, your chest, your anus, your genitals, your eyes, your ears, your heart, kidney, liver, spleen, and intestines. One of the things that I learned in sobriety is that so much of the existential anguish the alcoholic feels can just as easily be rectified by attending to basic physical needs. It sounds simple, and it is, but we're asked to evaluate what might be bothering us with the easy-to-remember acronym HALT, to see if we're hungry, anxious, lonely, or tired. Much tribulation can be solved not by recourse to some grand, ethereal, spiritual realm, but rather by eating, going for a walk, calling a friend, or taking a nap. Whether or not the mind can make a heaven of hell is one thing, but lunch certainly can. To those four possible diagnoses, I'd add having to take a shit, and between all of those possible afflictions I imagine that 90 percent of our emotional travails could be answered, at least momentarily. Satan's idealistic declaration is a young man's fantasy, but as entropy works her universal dictates it only becomes more apparent just how much of the world isn't an issue of attitude and positive thinking. There is the mind and there is the world, and how exactly they interact can be mysterious, but they are not the same thing. The mind can do many things, but material reality is not a matter of opinion.

And yet, it would be equivalently foolish to dismiss the strange, uncanny, eerie, and beautiful power of the imagination. Often the mind does seem as if it's its own place, and never so much than when in the act of creation, meditation, contemplation. Solipsism assumes—or maybe fears—an omniscience that is illusory, but it's true that the mind is something which can be tamed, something with power. Even if we're not masters of the universe, there is a sense in which we can occasionally master ourselves—or better yet, master those little universes which we occasionally create. Only a cruel sophist would pretend that the mind is so much of its own place that it could propel those who suffer away from Auschwitz, Hiroshima, My Lai, Bucha. To valorize consciousness at the expense of humanity is to countenance a nihilistic idolatry. Suffering has physical causes—so does mental suffering—and no amount of retreat can alter those circumstances, for material pain requires a material response. But only cynicism would deny the agency of imagination, the possibility that the mind can envision that which lays beyond, that the soul can orient itself toward a better world and in the process create something beautiful.

"Sorrow everywhere. Slaughter everywhere. If babies/ are not starving someplace, they are starving/somewhere else," writes Jack Gilbert in his incandescent *Collected Poems*. Despite the travesties and unrelenting horrors of life, Gilbert observes that there is "laughter/every day in the terrible streets of Calcutta,/and the women laugh in the cages of Bombay." The mind may not be its own place in the way that Bombay and Calcutta are, or Glasgow and Edinburgh, Bethlehem and London, New York and Pittsburgh, Auschwitz, Hiroshima, My Lai, and Bucha are, but for all of the pain that we encounter in our frail and fallen bodies there is still the possibility of joy, and the briefest and barest respite of such happiness can—sometimes— be enough. Gilbert offers an axiom, that if "we deny our happiness, resist our satisfaction,/we lessen the importance of their deprivation./We must resist delight. We can do without pleasure,/but not delight. Not enjoyment." In a rephrasing of Milton's contention, Gilbert maintains that "To make injustice the only/measure of our attention is to praise the Devil." And so I wonder, as Berkeley imagined worlds created by words, realities molded by his mind, as he enjoyed the cool sea breeze and the warm New England sun, what then did the slaves of Whitehall envision? What inner cosmos did they make with their minds?

Book XII—God

God does not exist. He is being itself beyond essence and existence. Therefore, to argue that God exists is to deny him.

—Paul Tillich, *Systematic Theology*

God Himself does not know what He is because he is not anything. Literally God *is not.*

—John Scotus Eriugena,
On the Division of Nature

Artillery Row is permeated with the overwhelming odor of shit and offal. Stumbling out past the gravestones of Bunhill Fields, I make my way down the street of densely packed, cross-timbered, thatched-roof homes, with families crowded into the upper stories and merchants plying their products below. It's only a year after the worst of the pandemic, and I note that few of the women and men making their way about Islington are covering their faces anymore, though, even if the disease no longer frightens, masks would be recommended against the putrid, rank miasma of cart-wielding butchers selling tripe and kidneys, of granulated soot from iron foundries down along the Thames, and of copious horse droppings; but these Londoners seem used to the olfactory assault. Occasionally a mist of roasting Arabica or walnuts comes from one of the coffee shops, but the predominant sense of the whole neighborhood is of stink so thick that it's like walking across the muddy floor of the river. More even than the dank smell of so much life crowded into these narrow streets there is a smoky scent, the burnt wooden frames of buildings a few blocks over just being cleared away now. I'm surrounded by a symphony of carpentry and masonry, all of London echoing with the chimes of a city that's being constructed anew. On some of the homes on Artillery Row workers sit on exposed wooden beams, the hammering taking on a rhythmic regularity as I absentmindedly walk in beat to the sound.

Throughout Islington there's a chorus of boisterous laughing and irritated yelling, drunken singing and the corner preaching of nonconformist ministers expelled from their pulpits. For all of that noise, there is a missing sound, the bells of St. Paul's mute for almost a year now, ever since the spire collapsed in the conflagration, though rumor has it that Christopher Wren has planned a massive, triumphant dome that will rise over the capital. Apparently the king, when he pays attention, is blanching at the cost. If I'm fascinated by these people, they give me no regard. I'm a refugee and exile in strange clothing, my torn and stained khakis, a red plaid button-down with the sleeves rolled up to my elbow, bits of straw sticking to my broken and brown untied suede shoes. Finally, I arrive at the house that was my destination, another cross-timbered cottage of black planks and white stucco, with small windows of opaque and bubbled glass. Mary appears at the heavy, black-painted oak door in her simple wool dress and flour-dusted apron, a few wisps of her father's chestnut hair escaping from her bonnet.

Wordlessly, she leads me into the house and down a dark, creaking hallway, scant squibs of light escaping in through the clouded windows in the front parlor, and we walk toward the back of the house where the dining room sits adjacent to the kitchen she's been in all day. A wooden table of uneven and dark-stained planks dominates the room, and it's clear that lunch was finished shortly before I arrived. A pewter plate frames the long spine of a salted cod, the luminescent tail and vacant-eyed head all that are left; a side dish has a bit of crust from some heavy, black bread and the rind of a dark orange cheddar. Crumbs of hardboiled egg yolk and bleached biscuit punctuate the table; the smell of watery ale's yeasty mustiness hangs damp in the room. The only bit of food which remains is a single, complete, bright red apple at the center of the table. Behind that table, on a rickety pew, sits John Milton.

Mary, gaze always cast down, simply nods her head and turns back into the kitchen. I uneasily sit down on the bench across from Milton, and finally, after so much of a wait, appraise the man for myself. Gaunter than I would have guessed, sclerosis-stooped in the manner of writers fortunate enough to reach this age, Milton is all angle and jutting bone, a threadbare brown shawl clipped over his sleight shoulders and his black woolen cloak, holes in his white stockings with a bit of pale, blue-veined flesh visible beneath, a pair of dusty gold buckled black shoes on his feet. He feels about on the table a bit, his cupped fingers springing over the knots of wood until he grasps the rough pottery of his ceramic mug, drawing it upward and taking a long, gurgling quaff of sudsy beer, before emitting a quiet but contented belch. Not far from the detritus of Milton's lunch is a small but thick quarto, its pages still a pristine and unwrinkled white, the paper as of yet uncut, and the frontispiece reading *Paradise Lost*. Three shillings over at Samuel Simmons's stall near St. Paul's, a run of some 1,300 copies, first released just this August of 1667. Sales so far are poor. Milton grasps about again on the table, until his hand lands on the cover of the book, and he lets his fingers shuffle through the pages while he seems to ever so faintly mumble something under his breath. I think it's the invocation of the poem, but I can't quite hear him. Thin-lipped and ashen, the most prominent feature of the poet's sallow-complexioned face are those slate-gray eyes, clouded over and the color of the North Sea before a storm. Milton stares toward some beyond that I can't see. His still-thick hair, however, remains the rich chestnut color that even the young women envied when he was just a boy in Latin school. We sit in a silence that feels as if it's about the space of half an hour, and at a point I wonder if he's even aware that I'm in the room with him. Finally, Milton speaks.

"You've traveled far, yes?"

"Not so far, I think," but Milton only seems to cluck with disapproval at that.

"What then do you think of this London right now?" he asks.

"It smells more than I would have guessed" is my honest response.

"Yes, the stench of libertinage, decadence, amorality, popery, and sin," he responds. Milton seems a man incapable of much joviality, and yet I feel like he's trying to restrain himself from curling those cadaverous lips into a grimace evidencing at least a bit of good cheer. Silence reenters, an awkwardness across centuries. Milton sounds like he's clearing his throat a bit, and then he speaks again.

"What then of London hence?" he asks, his curiosity unfeigned. And so I tell him. I explain how with even as huge as the city might be today, the million souls dispossessed of their homes in the country swarming into the metropolis as buildings arise along the Thames's banks and out toward the distant margins of London, that in the following century there will be even more people bounded into the capital. Factories, foundries, and forges will soon belch sulfury exhaust into the atmosphere, and Islington itself will be even more impoverished than it is today, people crowded among fetid tenements and working in the mills at every hour of the day. London itself, I explain to Milton, will be capital of a mighty but cruel empire, and not only shall a monarch remain on the throne in England, those same sovereigns will now govern with scepter and orb over the vast majority of the earth. Riches will flow into the city, tea from India and silk from China, cotton from the American South and diamonds from Africa. During the twentieth century,

London will nearly be destroyed by a monstrous evil out of central Europe, the Luftwaffe pummeling Islington into rubble, until in the postwar haze the English will rebuild it as a concrete labyrinth. Victorious but humbled in war, the British will lose their empire, but London itself will grow even bigger, more diverse, more alive. By my time, I explain, London is among the largest cities on earth, with every language heard, every religion practiced, every ethnicity, creed, and lifestyle evidenced. Milton, a nationalist but also a polyglot, a bigot but simultaneously a lover of liberty, seems to wearily consider that future.

"And what of God in this world?" he asks me.

"What of Him?"

"Does the Community of Saints still genuflect before the Lord? Do the martyrs still choose to die for Him? Do the faithful and pious still offer their prayers and supplications to Christ?" he asks me with a fervent intensity, leaning forward on his elbows a bit, corners of his mouth flecked with spittle.

"Our age has as many hypocrites as yours ever did, maybe even more, if that's what you're asking." He seems to consider my answer, nods after having found it a fair response, and leans back on the bench. I think on it a bit more, and decide that something else must be added.

"It's perhaps a disenchanted age, however. We know the price of everything and value of nothing, as a wag who lived two centuries after you put it. Our technology is awesome, unthinkably so. We've split the atom and released the elemental forces of the universe, to the point that it's now within humanity's capability to bring upon the apocalypse which you so feared and desired. Everything ever written, said, or even thought is available through a silicon oracle we all carry at every moment of the day, though wisdom hasn't improved. Communication is instantaneous but communion is rare. Comfort—even luxuriant comfort—is valorized beyond the sanctity of nature, and the gulfs between the richest and the poorest have become extreme in a way that you can't even envision. We've pushed ourselves to the precipice of ecological collapse because we worship an idol called the invisible hand. Transcendence, the numinous, the ecstatic, all are perilously rare experiences. If God ever walked with us in the cool of the evening, He doesn't anymore," I say with a bit more fire than I'd anticipated.

"And what of you? After all of this, what's your doxology?" Milton says. I brace myself a bit before I respond.

"I'm afraid that my own denominational *curriculum vitae* doesn't really shed light on what's in my heart, nor do I believe that it can for anyone, since the soul is a fickle and ever-mercurial thing," I evasively say. There is a throaty sound, almost a gurgle, from the poet, and it takes me a second to realize that he's laughing.

"In our epoch there is no choosing not to worship something," he says. I brace myself again.

"I was baptized in the Roman Catholic Church, have

confessed and taken communion in the Roman Catholic Church, and was married within the Roman Catholic Church." I must have been flinching slightly.

"There is no requirement to twinge in anticipation of some sort of thrashing," Milton says, his smile genuine. "If I could sup with Jesuits in Rome then surely I can sit here with you amidst the detritus of my midday meal."

"Well, when it comes to the actual doctrine of the Church," I apologize to somebody, "I'm fairly latitudinarian. I'd be considered a pretty bad Catholic, by any estimation. Here's my personal theological checklist: transubstantiation—doubtful; the trinity—inscrutable; apostolic succession—why not?; papal infallibility—absolutely not; original sin—obviously; the incarnation—absolutely, at least the poetics of the thing."

"So many words to say 'heretic,'" Milton says, and it's unclear if he's joking or not; if his appraisal is because I'm too much of a Catholic or not enough.

"How many words did you use in *De Doctrina Christiana?*"

"Ah, fair enough," Milton answers, "but nobody here knows about any of that yet."

"Look," I say to him, "I actually find myself in the most Lutheran of positions, priest in a Church of one, though I'd like to get it retrofitted with stained glass, kneelers, and devotional statues. Being a bit all over the place religiously is hardly an uncommon predicament, since in some ways Americans are a particularly spiritually promiscuous people, that whole Emersonian pose which is the greatest legacy of the Reformation." He leans back a bit again, and seems to focus his cloudy eyes on me as best he can.

"Well, a man may be a heretic in the truth, and if he believes things only because his pastor says so, without knowing other reason, the very truth he holds becomes his heresy," Milton says.

After a pause, I say, "You know, I've never been confirmed, which sometimes I regret because I wouldn't mind being able to choose my own name, but I'm not that much of a completist. I informally attended a synagogue in college and I'm strongly considering fully converting to Judaism (I still might), interested in part because of patrilinear ancestry a few generations back. For a while I thought that I might become a Unitarian, but the local church didn't respond to my emails, and that's really the extent of it," I explain.

"Goodness," Milton says, "A papist, a Pharisee, and a pagan, what strange vegetables you Americans grow in your distant future."

"I'm not an atheist, you know. Everybody assumes that my irreverence, my profanation, my blasphemies, my heresies mean that I'm an atheist, but I'm not."

"Oh?" he says, and whether it's politeness or disinterest I'm unsure, but I continue anyhow.

"Other than some performative high school cynicism, I never really went atheist because it's boring, and agnosticism (which while perhaps epistemologically correct to my own confession) is just bourgeois atheism. High Church Anglicanism has its appeal to me, but for class and cultural reasons it would be anathema to go Protestant, though like many I'm struck by the quandary that the American Catholic Church has such abominable politics by comparison."

"So, you'd keep all the bones and rags, the relics and icons, the superstitious ephemera of the Whore of Babylon, when the living word of God speaks through scripture clearly to the most faithful of man?" For the first time Milton sounds not just bemused in his condescension, but actually angry.

"When it comes to lower church positions," I tell him, "I'm with Stephen Dedalus in James Joyce's *The Portrait of the Artist as a Young Man:* 'What kind of liberation would that be to forsake an absurdity which is logical and coherent and to embrace one which is illogical and incoherent?'" Milton seems, in the moment, too confused to be offended.

"Mere aestheticism," he says, dismissively flapping his hand as if to shoo me away, crossing his arms in front of the rough wool of his shawl and turning toward the iron-latticed window letting scant light into the dining room from the small garden out back.

"I don't begrudge that evaluation—sometimes I dismiss it as mere aestheticism as well. What can I say? I'm (technically) Catholic, I don't dismiss aesthetics lightly."

"Truth and understanding are not such wares as to be monopolized and traded in by tickets and statuettes and standards," Milton says. "We must not think to make a staple commodity of all the knowledge in the land, to mark and license it like our broadcloth and our woolpacks."

"Look," I begin, "despite my apostasies, my heresies, and my blasphemies I do unironically respect and adhere to that reasoning, my faith is of a particular type. Not a single word of the Nicene Creed, the Apostles' Creed, or the Athanasian Creed can be read by me in any conventional way; the *Pater Noster* more enigma than prayer, the *Ave Maria* poetry as much as supplication. Still, we are what we are."

"And with that litany of all that we don't believe, then what are we, Dr. Simon?" Milton asks, the first time that he's acknowledged me by name.

"In general, I err on the side of high church rather than low, the allegorical rather than the literal, poetry rather than theology."

"If you exclude those burnt spices and infernal bells from the church, then I can ascent to the primrose fragrance of allegory instead, the sweet harmonies of poetry as well," Milton says.

In response, I shuffle my feet and tell the poet, "I'm jaded enough to hold to that impulse that it's best to tend to our own garden, I have my moments of utopian enthusiasm as well, and I think that the millennium is a beautiful story rather than a reality."

"I still fully expect it to happen," Milton simply says.

There is another silence.

"So, what of you then? We've debated what you've believed

for centuries now, thousands of books and monographs spent on arguing whether you were a Calvinist or an Arminian, tenured careers made over the issue of if you're a materialist or an idealist, entry into the canon based on if you're of the Devil's party or not—so where then do you stand, Milton?"

His wrinkled, liver-spotted hand, with ragged cuticle and uncut nails lingers over the crust of black bread, finally filching it from the plate, and drawing it into his mouth. Milton loudly chews, and while swallowing he picks up the new copy of *Paradise Lost*, and thumbs through its paper, though he of course can't see his own words on the page.

"So down they sat," Milton began from memory, "And to thir viands fell, nor seemingly / The Angel, nor in mist, the common gloss / Of Theologians, but with keen dispatch / Of real concoctive heate / To transubstantiate."

"Book V," I say.

"And for what reason, in your apparent proclaimed deep knowledge of my poem, would I choose such a word as 'transubstantiate?'"

"To keep the editors of *Milton Studies* in business?" He doesn't laugh. Milton clears his throat again.

"'What redounds, transpires / Through Spirts with ease; nor wonder; if by fire / Of sooty coal the Empiric Alchimist / Can turn, or holds it possible to turn / Metals of drossiest Ore to perfet Gold / As from the Mine.' That is why, of course. Your imagination is simply too small," England's greatest poet says to me.

"Come again, then?"

"To transubstantiate, your Eucharistic piffle, the Bread God of the papists, you assume this one moment is when the divine presence appears, but what you must understand is that the sacred *is always coming into this world*."

I sit, quiet. Milton continues after a beat:

"My disagreement is that the divinity doesn't wait for wafer and wine to transform into the body and blood of Christ, because our cosmos is *forever turning back and forth into God.*" Stunned for a minute, and I answer Milton.

"You're not a Protestant after all, you're a pantheist. So where is God then?" I ask. The poet pauses, gathering his thoughts, opening *Paradise Lost* and thumbing through the pages of that cosmos of a volume.

"There is no more eternity than there is right now," Milton says, "and no more paradise than the place in which you sit. It has not been lost. If you seek paradise, it is right here and right now."

"And is heaven empty of its ruler?" I ask. I genuinely want to know. With what seems to be the first genuine smile I've seen on him, Milton offers a not unkind laugh.

"Even if the only Lord is the God of imagination, He is no less powerful and good and true and beautiful and sacred and holy because of that. And so it is, and so it is, and so it is," Milton says as he continues to repeat himself, shutting this book which you're now finishing.

OTHER
BOOKMARKED TITLES

Virginia Woolf's *Mrs. Dalloway*
by Robin Black

Middlemarch and the Imperfect Life
by Pamela Erens

James Baldwin's *Another Country*
by Kim McLarin

Truman Capote's *In Cold Blood*
by Justin St. Germain

Vladimir Nabokov's *Speak, Memory*
by Sven Birkerts

William Stoner and the Battle for the Inner Life
by Steve Almond

Stephen King's "The Body"
by Aaron Burch

Raymond Carver's *What We Talk About When We Talk About Love*
by Brian Evenson

(For a complete series list, go to
https://www.igpub.com/category/titles/bookmarked/)